RETROSPECTIVE
Recollections of a Montreal Art Dealer

William R. Watson

RETROSPECTIVE

Recollections of a Montreal Art Dealer

University of Toronto Press

Toronto and Buffalo
Printed in Canada
Reprinted in 2018

ISBN 0-8020-2148-4
ISBN 978-1-4875-8573-0 (paper)
LC 74-75586

The preparation and publication of this book were assisted by grants from the Canada Council.

To my wife, Cecile
and to my daughters
Claire and Louise

Contents

Foreword

The events and impressions recalled and recounted in this little book were written by the author in his eighty-fifth year.

Through the years his wife and his artist friends had expressed the hope that he would write his memoirs, but he was always reluctant to do so. He did not consider himself a literary man, observing that his writings would be only light-hearted recollections of a happy life. And so they are. They also reflect an era, an important time in the development of Canadian art, and reveal a civilized mind, a generous heart, and an imaginative and colourful character whose spirit was seldom daunted.

The reminiscences were never intended to be the story of his life as a man. Indeed they do not fully reveal his devotion to his family, his knowledge and love of the classics, of music, of the sea, of his constant study and loving observation of nature, nor of course the flaws, inherent in such a forceful personality. He was an uncommon man with a vitality and a positive approach to life which touched all who knew him.

In his latter years he responded to the urging of family and friends, aware of the part he had played in our cultural development, and so he was finally persuaded to write his story.

Claire Watson
Louise Slemin

Preface

These random reminiscences are not intended to be a story of the times nor of my life as a man. They are nearer to being a factual record of a fascinating profession that was new in Canada.

Through it runs the thread of many happy friendships with those artists whose work I admired, exhibited and sold.

William R. Watson
Montreal
September 1972

RETROSPECTIVE
Recollections of a Montreal Art Dealer

I

Arrival in Montreal

1905

It was by common ordinary luck that I became an art dealer. I had wanted to be an artist and to this end I had studied art in Liverpool for more than a year, but apparently made no progress. I did, however, read a great deal about art and artists, in particular *Modern Painters* by John Ruskin, and here I came across a definition that made me put aside my brushes. It was: 'Art is not the transcription of anything, but its transmutation' – and there and then the world lost another third-rate artist. I began to think of other things, other ways to remain in the world of art – to work in a museum, or an art gallery. My father had said, 'some frustrated artists become art critics,' a sarcasm which I much appreciated later on in life. But I was still haunted by dreams of somehow living in the world of art. It had been a vague wish from an early age, and I now understand the influences of my childhood.

I was brought up in a house that was almost a museum. My father, prosperous as a Liverpool jute merchant, was well able to indulge his ardent love for antiques and works of art by filling our house with them. They ranged from Chippendale furniture, Chelsea, Derby, Wedgewood and Chinese porcelain, to miniatures on ivory, kept in the many cabinets in our home. He had an extensive library on antiques and was an astute collector, buying in all parts of England wherever there was an auction or the sale of an estate. In our house there were also many paintings, and I found myself more interested in them than anything else. As I remember the paintings from this end of the long corridor of time, I think now they were the heel of his collection, imbued with a prettiness and perhaps a 'kiss Mama' sentimentality. I have often thought since that, inasmuch as they were the works of contemporary English artists, some of whom lived in Liverpool, my father had bought them through a sincere wish to encourage their painters, something I was destined to do for artists in another country.

The Boer War in 1899 was disastrous for jute merchants who had firm contracts without 'Acts of God or War' clauses for protection. World prices soared, contracts were fulfilled at great loss, and my father apparently faced financial ruin. He carried on until 1905. Then with the encouragement and financial assistance of his fairly wealthy brother, the poet Sir William Watson, he decided to move to Canada with his magnificent collection of antiques. 'It will also be a land of opportunity for my four young sons,' he said.

I arrived in Montreal on October 10, 1905. Being the eldest son, I had come a month ahead of my family to find a furnished apartment for them. By chance, on leaving the ship, I walked up St François Xavier Street. There I saw a small art shop with a portrait by the French artist Jean Jacques Henner in the window. I returned the next day to see more of the place. It was owned by John Ogilvy, whom I later learned was the only exclusive art dealer in Montreal, that is to say, the only dealer selling only paintings and no other goods. He was a tall, dignified Scotsman with white hair and sideburns, and I felt somewhat shy in his towering presence. Diffidently, I asked to see some Canadian paintings, expecting to see portraits of Indians in a landscape, though at that time I knew nothing of Paul Kane, Cornelius Krieghoff or F.A. Verner. To my surprise he said he had no Canadian pictures, but showed me a bronze, *Soupir du Lac*, by Philippe Hébert, a Montreal sculptor. I told Mr Ogilvy I was interested in art and if possible would like to work in his gallery. He appeared to be surprised, and asked me how old I was, and how long I had been in Canada. I said I was eighteen, and had been in Canada since yesterday. He looked at me with appraising steady blue eyes, and said, 'Well, young fellow, perhaps I can do something for you.' In a few minutes I found myself engaged as office boy, floor-sweeper, and general manager of his little gallery at the princely salary of $10 a week. To my astonishment he gave me the keys before asking my name or where I lived, and then told me to take the names of callers, close up at 5.30 PM and open at 9 AM. 'I'll see you in the morning,' he said, and left. I boldly began to rearrange a few pictures and get rid of some accumulated dust. I was singing with happiness, and wondering what my father would say when I told him on his arrival that I had already got a job, and, more particularly, was doing exactly what I had hoped to do.

The gallery, I discovered, had been established in 1897, and was actually a sort of hobby for Mr Ogilvy, who had settled in Montreal after retiring from a successful dry goods business in western Canada. When I met him he was nearly eighty years of age, and spent only a few hours in his gallery each day, and anyone buying a picture had to take it away himself. The gallery was not large, had only a small selection of paintings, and was furnished in a simple fashion. It was opposite the Montreal Stock Exchange, and it appeared that most visitors were brokers or brokers' clients, who called Mr Ogilvy 'Uncle John,' and often dropped in for a leisurely chat. He was one of the founders of the St James's Club and was known by all its members for his talent as a clubman, and for his enjoyment of conversation, good food, and the wines of a connoisseur. He was an inveterate cigar smoker, but as far as I knew he never bought any. It was the privilege of his friends to say, 'Sir John, would you like a cigar?' He never refused, and he smoked them until he held the butt on a pin.

The paintings we sold were contemporary French, English, and Dutch, sent from England by Harry Wallis, an art dealer in London. I persuaded Mr Ogilvy that we should not put glass on oil paintings. For over a hundred years this had been the custom, to protect them from the greasy film left by oil lamps and gas lights.

I had now been in Canada about a year and I sincerely wished to become a Canadian in every respect. I wanted to read its history, its literature, and to encourage its artists to the best of my ability, if I ever had a gallery of my own. I felt happy one morning to tell Mr Ogilvy that I had sold my first picture by a Canadian artist, *Roses in a Glass Bowl* by F.S. Coburn. I also soon sold the Philippe Hébert *Soupir du Lac* and hoped that Mr Ogilvy would allow me some freedom in taking Canadian paintings on consignment. I suggested we could charge the artist 20 per cent commission, but I made no progress in this, as he thought most Canadian paintings 'too noisy to mix with quiet Dutch pictures.' Consequently we had very few Canadian paintings, for only those painted in the Dutch nineteenth century tradition appealed to him even though he had approved of Coburn's still-life paintings and had been pleased with my first sale.

I don't remember how much business we did; perhaps a few thousand dollars a year. There was only a single book to record the paintings we bought, and these entries were crossed out when the paintings were sold. Business then was simple. There was no income tax, no sales tax, no forms of any kind to fill out – what was sold was your own affair, and as confidential as a love letter.

I still feel a great affection for that grand old man, John Ogilvy, and I saw him often until he died at a very great age. His attitude to me was always such that I might have been his grandson. The year he retired, in 1908, he took me to England and introduced me to all the art dealers from whom he had purchased paintings. He sought their support for me, so that I could obtain almost any paintings I wished. My credit was to be as good as his had been – a very comfortable situation, and I took full advantage of it. In a further example of his generosity and confidence in me, he said, 'Any pictures that remain unsold when we close up, you may have on consignment and pay me as you sell them.' I thus inherited a business begun as a hobby in 1897.

2

Early Years

1908-1921

Shortly after my father's arrival in Canada in 1905, he established the Watson Antique Gallery on Peel Street. The antiques which had furnished our home in Liverpool were shipped from England and formed the basis of the collection he sold from his shop. Montreal 'society' was then very pro-English, and the shop was an immediate success, soon involving two of my brothers and my eldest sister. It was on the ground floor of one of several large houses which had been converted to commercial premises. The decor was plush velvet and comfortable, and with the large and important collection of antiques, it almost looked like a museum exhibition.

When I returned from my first buying trip to England, my father agreed to rent me some separate space in his shop. Mr Ogilvy warmly approved of the arrangements I was making, and wished me the best of luck. He assured me that Peel Street was a better situation than St François Xavier for an art dealer, for while St François Xavier was in the old section of Montreal, running from the docks to the financial section, Peel was near the railway stations and the shopping area along Ste Catherine Street.

As a young art dealer I soon discovered that some of my father's antique buyers could also be interested in paintings. In 1908, business was flourishing in Montreal, and Dominion Square was a busy centre of town. Most of the old houses on the west side of Peel Street had been converted into stores. On the southeast corner of Ste Catherine Street stood a church (Erskine Presbyterian), and on the east side of the square was the YMCA where the Sun Life Insurance building is today. Business was slowly moving uptown from St James, Craig, and Notre Dame Streets. It is hard to believe that in 1910 my father was offered the two-storey building we occupied on Peel Street for $9,000. He asked for time to think about it, as he was leaving for Europe on a buying trip. When he returned the owner had died, and his two sons had withdrawn it from the market. It later became Child's Restaurant and the site is now probably worth over a million dollars. This illustrates what happens to the value of property in a fast-growing city like Montreal, and perhaps explains half the fortunes made in North America at the beginning of this century.

In those days Montreal seemed to be a predominantly English-speaking city, which surprised those visitors who had always heard Quebec called 'French Canada.' From the days of the early fur traders business had been largely in English or Scottish hands, and this British influence was still to be seen. Practically all the stores west of Bleury Street had English names, and few French-Canadians were really wealthy or had capital available. A great many still lived in the country, and their drift to the city was relatively slow.

For some time French- and English-speaking mayors had been elected alternately, which seemed to be a pleasant arrangement. I had met a former mayor, Sir William Hingston, on board the ship which brought me from England. One evening in the lounge he had talked to the immigrant passengers about Canada and Montreal. A well-beloved surgeon, Sir William died in 1907, two years after my arrival.

At that time, one of the most beautiful and impressive buildings in the city was the Bank of Montreal, which had been built on Place d'Armes in 1847. It was later enlarged and the restoration was completed in 1905, the year I arrived. The magnificent columns of polished green granite gave the interior a solid richness of character. I often took my art dealer friends from abroad to see this building and they always marvelled at the splendour of the interior which resembled that of a Roman basilica. It was, I believe, the most monumental bank building in the world. As a young man, I was so impressed with the huge columns and their renaissance style that I imagined their being shipped from Italy across the Atlantic Ocean, which if true would have been a feat equal to bringing Cleopatra's Needle to London. In fact, they came from a quarry in Vermont.

Montreal seemed to be growing day by day. In those days it was a comfortable city, with a population of about 400,000, with wide spaces, such as Place d'Armes, Victoria Square, Dominion Square and Phillips Square, and tree-lined streets with the mountain in the background. It was pleasantly alive with the clip-clop of horses in summer and the cheerful jingle of sleigh bells in winter, and the clang of streetcar bells, which created an atmosphere of life and gaiety. There was a great deal of merrymaking. Good Scotch whiskey was fifteen cents a drink and beer ten cents a bottle. People relied almost entirely on themselves for entertainment and celebrated winter as a time for outdoor fun, holding annual 'fêtes' and erecting a magnificent Ice Palace on Dominion Square. At night, snowshoe club members marched through the nearly empty streets in picturesque costumes, with jolly bugle bands, on their way to Mount Royal, climbing over it to an inn called 'Lumpkins.' I recall that snow used to be carried down from the mountain and thrown onto the streets at intersections to ease the horses' loads. Many streets had wooden sidewalks. The first movie house in Montreal, at Bleury and Ste Catherine Streets, was opened about 1910. It was called the Nickelodeon and for five cents we could see 'The Perils of Pauline.'

At this time (1910) the Art Association of Montreal's gallery on Phillips Square was holding almost continuous exhibitions. This was actually the first art gallery in Canada, and predated the Metropolitan Museum of Art in New York City; it contributed to Montreal's reputation as one of the most cultured cities in North America. In fact, as early as 1826 there had been an Art Society in Montreal which gave prizes to artists, and in 1847 a group of citizens and artists formed The Montreal Society of Artists. The Art Association itself was incorporated in 1860, but did not have a permanent gallery until nearly twenty years later. Then a prominent Montreal citizen, Benaiah Gibb, bequeathed his land on the east side of Phillips Square to the association, which erected a rather attractive building on the site.

It was officially opened in May 1879 by the Marquis of Lorne, the husband of Princess Louise who exhibited some of her own paintings at the opening. From that time on, the Art Association's gallery flourished remarkably, and made increasing contact with the public. The free-for-all Spring Show was held there, and the Royal Canadian Academy had many exhibitions in its halls. Here, in this interesting building with its winding wooden stairway, there were exhibitions of paintings by William Brymner, Horatio Walker, Albert Robinson, Clarence Gagnon, J.C. Franchère, M.A. Suzor Côté, Maurice Cullen, F.S. Coburn, Henri Julien, J.W. Morrice, and many other members of the Academy. During such exhibitions, tea was served by the lady members on Wednesdays and Saturdays, contributing to the general relaxed and pleasant atmosphere.

Other generous contributions to this building came from many business and professional men who were patrons of the arts. Some of their names should still arouse our profound gratitude: James Ross, the railway builder; Elwood Hosmer and E.B. Greenshields; Huntley Redpath Drummond, the industrialist; Richard B. Angus, the banker; Dr William Gardner, who was president of the Art Association of Montreal in 1903; Dr Francis Shepherd, the great surgeon, and of course, Sir William Van Horne, the builder of the CPR. These gentlemen were always willing to show their own private collections to interested art lovers.

All these activities formed part of the art world with which I began to feel involved, even to becoming art critic, first for the daily *Witness* and then for the Montreal *Gazette*. Being art critic and art dealer at the same time was always interesting. Invitations to 'tea for the new Morrice' would bring me among those groups of collectors who celebrated their new acquisitions as a social event, and the exhibitions at the Art Association's gallery brought me in contact with our local artists.

Around 1910, the old Holton property at the corner of Sherbrooke Street West and Ontario Avenue was bought by the Art Association for $70,000. J.W. Morrice had painted the old Holton house prior to its demolition, and this work is still on view in the present gallery, now called the Montreal Museum of Fine Arts. Remarkably, this noble museum, with its magnificent Greek facade and marble stairs, was built and furnished out of member subscriptions alone.

On the night of December 9, 1912, at a grand inaugural ball, I heard the Governor-General, the Duke of Connaught, declare the building open to the public. I remember seeing displayed for that occasion many paintings from the private collections of Montrealers, who arrived for the grand opening either in horse-drawn carriages or in new automobiles. Far more important exhibitions could now be organized, as there was ample wall space and splendid lighting. The space was also suitable for concerts and other cultural activities, and for the establishment of an art library of considerable importance. It is worth repeating that the building of this new gallery was financed by a group of Montreal's dedicated art lovers, who were also proud of their city, and anxious to contribute to its beauty, and to encourage a more vital way of life. A new era of dignity and beauty had begun.

In the meantime, from my one-room 'gallery' on Peel Street, I was beginning to sell Canadian paintings and bronzes. But I still had to go to Europe every year for the inevitable quota of Dutch School unabashed 'pretty pictures,' or quite obviously be unable to continue in business.

One of the discriminating people who came into our shop from time to time was Sir William Van Horne, who used to walk leisurely down Peel Street on the way to his office. He bought carved jade and ivory from my father, who once persuaded him to look over my paintings. I heard him describe them with one word – 'trash.' I instantly learned something about relativity. Of course, compared to his great collection of Dutch old masters, my *Mother and Child* by the Dutch artist Josef Israels might have seemed exactly that. But I was too young to be crushed. I still thought Israels was a sincere, honest, and good painter.

Sir William Van Horne's collection had a world-wide reputation. However, I imagine it is not well known that he himself was a good artist, far beyond the average part-time painter, and he was certainly the most knowledgeable of Montreal's art collectors. His interests ranged from Chinese and Japanese ivories and ceramics to almost anything fine. He was always generous in allowing interested people to visit his collection. On one occasion, about 1907, he invited me to come to his house for breakfast, to see two paintings by Frans Hals that he had just acquired, and to meet Rudyard Kipling.

As a young man, I was, of course, excited about meeting Kipling, and as an art dealer about seeing the Hals. Perhaps breakfast was the wrong meal, the wrong time to meet Kipling, for I remember my disappointment with his cold taciturnity and his sharp beetle-browed glance through steel-rimmed spectacles. In his morning mood he said a few things about the weather, and immediately after breakfast he vanished. Sir William remained to show me the two magnificent portraits, and walked around his home with me to see a part of his impressive collection. I noticed one unusual landscape which appeared to be French in style and was signed 'Enroh Nav.' When I said I had never heard of the artist, Sir William smiled and said, 'Well, read the signature backwards.' We had a good laugh. Later on he showed me more of his works. I saw his impressive painting of *Sydney Steel Mills at Night* and also many of his perceptive delicate water colors of Japanese vases, and various sketches.

His top-floor room was a sanctuary, his paint box beside the inevitable cigar box. He would talk of Ming and T'ang, and although apparently not suffering fools gladly never made my ignorance feel heavier than it was. I have often thought that it was the imagination that made him an artist and collector that also made him the great railroad builder. He must have enjoyed the dramatic action when in 1885 he had stood near his friend Donald Smith (Lord Strathcona) and watched him drive the last spike joining the CPR to the Pacific. It was like the signing of a finished painting.

Another Montreal collector who should not be forgotten for his contribution to the culture of his time and his city was Sir George Drummond, president of the Bank of Montreal. Like Van Horne, he was always willing to show his paintings to interested visitors, and I heard a revealing story concerning one of these occasions. He had been showing a group of visiting school teachers his really fine collection, paintings by Corot, Gainsborough, Turner, and many others. Then, as they were leaving, the spokesman of the party turned to him and said, 'Could you tell us, sir, where the originals of these paintings are?' There is no record of Sir George's reply, but he is known to have been an extremely good-natured man.

Several private collectors thus contributed to Montreal's cultural fame, but what of our national status? I had often wondered what Canada's National Gallery would be like, since Montreal had such comparative splendour. So about 1910, as a last assignment in my capacity as art critic for the *Gazette*, I went to Ottawa to write a report on the National Gallery. I had vaguely considered this edifice might be an approximate equivalent to the Metropolitan Museum in New York, so I was quite taken aback when the desk clerk at the Russell House Hotel, where I was staying, said he had never heard of it. A policeman on the street denied all knowledge of it, but suggested that James Wilson, an art dealer on Sparks Street, might know. Mr Wilson, who sold prints and frames, was indeed able to give me careful directions, and I was soon standing in front of a building on O'Connor Street that bore the number he had indicated. A rather large sign across the front of it read, 'Marine and Fisheries Building, Government Fisheries Exhibit.' I pushed open the door, and the effect was startling. On the left was a brilliant red channel-marking gas-buoy, looking really formidable out of the water, and about ten feet to the right of this dominating object stood a full sized plaster replica of the Venus de Milo. This, I took it, was to indicate that art had a half-share interest with the fisheries department. Indeed, the fisheries had the better half, for they occupied the whole of the ground floor except for the Venus. On the immediate right of the dusty statue was a steep wooden stairway, at the base of which was a painted sign, 'National Gallery,' with a hand pointing upward.

At the top of the stairs was an oak panelled door. When I opened it, a bell on a coiled spring jangled. This caused some action, for a somewhat elderly woman appeared from behind a counter on the left, and I politely asked if I could have a catalogue. She gave me a printed sheet of paper, which was apparently the total inventory of our national art treasures. I was the sole occupant of that one large room for more than an hour. The pictures were hung in a crowded fashion, one above the other, and were covered with glass, most of them with elaborate gold frames. The light was from a central skylight.

I still remember some of the titles: *Dolly at the Sabot Makers* (William Brymner); the sad scene of *Mortgaging the Homestead* (George Reid); the coyness of *A Little Puritan* (Franklin Brownell); the pretty Victorian sweetness of *The Flower Girl* (by the Russian artist Alexis Harlamoff); the nostalgic *A Summer Idyll* (Edmund Wyly Grier), and the sudden surprise of seeing a copy of *The Death of Wolfe* by Benjamin West, later replaced in 1918 by the original which had been painted in 1770. Perhaps half the Canadian works were diploma pictures given by members of the Royal Canadian Academy. There was nothing of international significance, and the total impression of our National Gallery was that it was far from being worthy of its name. Nothing much had happened in the thirty years since its founding by the Marquis of Lorne, our fourth governor-general, and the Princess Louise, who had done so much for art in Canada.

Our first national 'gallery' had actually been a room in the Clarendon Hotel in Ottawa, where through the initiative of the Marquis of Lorne an exhibition of pictures by members of the Royal Canadian Academy was held in 1880. After he returned to England, apparently the gallery languished, for it was certainly the ugly duckling of government finance as I saw it in 1910. It was not until 1913 that it received official status through an Act of Parliament under the Ministry of Public Works. A prime supporter of the bill presented to the House of Commons was the unrelenting Sir Edmund Walker, who became the first chairman of the gallery's Board of Trustees. Then came the appointment of a professional director, Eric Brown. From that time it made steady progress, especially in the direction of supporting Canadian art and artists, notably the Group of Seven in its time of struggle. It now became easier for me to persuade the public to follow the example of the National Gallery.

Around 1913 the Montreal art collections consisted almost entirely of works by European artists. A dry goods merchant and prominent citizen, E.B. Greenshields, in 1906 had written an authoritative book entitled *Landscape Painting and Modern Dutch Artists*, which I saw on sale even in Amsterdam. It was perhaps this popular book which had such influence in maintaining an interest in Dutch art in Montreal, an influence which prevailed for so long and was so difficult to supplant. Indeed, for many years my customers would look only at Canadian paintings which resembled those of the nineteenth century Dutch artists so highly praised in Greenshields' book. Few Canadian artists were able to make more than a tolerable living, and most of them did this by teaching, through commercial illustration, or by making etchings which could be sold for a few dollars. The portrait painters were the most fortunate, although William Notman, the exceptional Montreal photographer, was making things more difficult for them year by year.

An important event of the time was the founding in 1912 of the Arts

Club at a meeting in Maurice Cullen's studio on Beaver Hall Hill, one of the declared purposes being 'to bring together those interested in the arts in all its branches.' And so it did.

In my own little show-room at the back of my father's shop on Peel Street I had begun to carry out what I had told Mr Ogilvy I wished to do, that is, everything possible to support Canadian artists. In a short time I had paintings by F.S. Coburn, J.C. Franchère, Henri Julien, Maurice Cullen, Suzor Côté, Paul Caron, and Clarence Gagnon, and sketches by James Wilson Morrice. I visited artists' studios and bought from them, or if agreeable took paintings on consignment, in which case they were sold for 20 per cent commission; I sometimes bought from the annual exhibitions of the Art Association of Montreal, especially in the Spring Show. My father agreed that I could put Canadian paintings in our small window and this attracted some buyers. It is interesting that snow landscapes were the most difficult to sell, perhaps because they were too far removed from the classic 'brown' Dutch landscapes.

In my search for Canadian paintings, I had come to know and admire several of our artists. One of these was Morrice, who was fortunate in having independent means and thus being able to spend a large part of his time in Europe, where his paintings were much appreciated. He returned to Montreal quite frequently to see his family and friends and to paint the winter, which he always contended was our most beautiful season. 'The summer is too green and the autumn is too pretty,' he used to say.

Once in 1908 he allowed me to sit beside him, while he painted a winter view down Peel Street, as seen from a window in the old part of the Windsor Hotel. It was a 10 × 14 inch panel and took him about two hours to complete, and was immediately bought by one of his patrons, Dr Francis Shepherd. More than forty years later I was amazed to see it again, and to be able to buy it for my own little collection of Canadian art. It is a treasured possession in every way.

At this time Morrice was the only Canadian artist who had achieved an international reputation. In Montreal his paintings had been sold for many years by his friend, John Heaton of Scott and Sons Art Gallery, a firm established on Notre Dame Street in the early part of the century.

From the time I first met Morrice, I often thought of writing my impressions of him, and this I did more than twenty years later in an article for the Montreal *Gazette*. Here is this account, written in 1932:

I first met J.W. Morrice in 1906 during one of his periodical visits to Montreal. He was then very keen on painting some of the winter aspects of the city; and the morning he came into the gallery on St François Xavier Street, he had been making a sketch of Bonsecours Church. While he sat warming his hands at the fire, he complained of the difficulty of working outdoors, in the cold – how the paint stiffened, the hands grew numb and inflexible so that one 'could hardly feel what was being painted.' Since then, that exceptional phrase 'feel what was being painted' has recurred to me very often when looking at his pictures. His fluent technique leads one to believe that the very play of the brush was a pleasure to him. There is always the feeling too of the sheer joy of creating on canvas. The phrase is probably worth recording as one of those flashes that illuminate a whole background of life and purpose.

A few days later he came again into the gallery smiling broadly, a sketch box in his pocket and a camera in his hand. He then told the story, which was evidently a great joke to him, of how a lady friend, solicitous for his comfort, had presented him with the camera so that he need no longer bother to go sketching in the cold. 'She tells me,' he said, 'that all I have to do now is press this ... and there you are!' The idea of Morrice using a camera is at least humorous.

I think it was 1910 in Paris, when we spent an evening together that is memorable. The city was excited over Edmond Rostand's new play, 'Chantecler,' and our conversation came around to it and its 'original' conception of animals and birds symbolizing humanity. 'No,' said Morrice, 'that idea antedates Christ ... why Aristophanes did that in his play, "The Birds." Listen to this ...' and he quoted long passages from Aristophanes in classic Greek, and compared them with others in 'Chantecler.'

The ardour for life and enthusiasm for all its manifestations was most inspiring when Morrice was at his best. One could not remain long with him without discovering the depth and profundity of his mind, and the exquisiteness of his taste both in literature and art. Perhaps Rembrandt, Velasquez, and Goya could be considered his trinity of old masters, and among the modern men Manet and Boudin had a special appeal, while he had great admiration for the work of the American artist Prendergast. Personally I think Prendergast was a great influence.

Morrice had a profound knowledge and a genuine love of music. He admired Beethoven and Bach. He could play the flute for hours. His memory, we may be sure, was exceptional. He told me that he could recall a particular scene clearly enough to paint it years after he had actually seen it; and I remember his having recited the whole of Thompson's 'City of Dreadful Night' from memory.

He loved a good story, and to hear his musical laughter was infectious jollity. In conversations on art, his own views were very difficult to discover. He would rather paint than talk about art. What he had to say, he said in paint. Perhaps his reticently-given opinions would be confined to a phrase, such as ... 'general principles are futile, ... there are no final conclusions.' Morrice, with his genuinely aristocratic mind, accepted that art to the multitude was an esoteric thing quite beyond their comprehension. That a few discriminating critics and friends should appreciate his work seemed entirely sufficient to him.

Morrice was of course fortunate in that he did not have to paint for his living, but purely for the happiness of self-expression and to gratify the inner urge to create. Consequently most of his pictures are lyrical, and sprang from a pure esthetic emotion. It was always difficult to get to see his innumerable sketches, yet in his studio they were scattered about in the most inconsequential way. Only a few of them were ever carried to completion in a subsequent picture.

There is an entry in the Journal of Arnold Bennett, who was a friend of Morrice's, which is worth quoting: 'Tuesday, May 16, 1905 – Morrice dined with me and stayed till one AM. He has the joy of life in a high degree, and he likes living alone. "I enjoy everything," he said. "I got up this morning and I saw an old woman walking along, and she was the finest old woman I ever did see. She was a magnificent old woman, and I was obliged to make a sketch of her."'

If an artist's attitude to his art could be explained in nine words, it is contained in that significant phrase, 'I was obliged to make a sketch of her.' What more can be said than Morrice felt like that?

At the time he did the Peel Street sketch he was forty-two, and I was only twenty-one, but he was kind and indulgent, and made me feel comfortable in his company despite the difference in our ages. His appearance somehow reminded me of a certain portrait of Shakespeare; when he was playing his flute in his studio in Paris he seemed like Pan; when he was reciting poetry he became an actor.

He knew that I was hoping to do something for our neglected

Canadian artists, and he applauded my appreciation of Maurice Cullen. Morrice promised me that if I ever had a gallery of my own he would let me have some of his sketches. He kept his word, and I often brought back from Paris a number of these delightful, spontaneous works. I should mention that, suitably framed, these sketches sold in those days for $90. Morrice was perhaps only a casual friend, for I did not see him very often, but I liked him to the point of reverence.

Another artist I knew at this time was William Brymner, the great teacher. He was a Scotsman born in Greenock, but (to paraphrase Stephen Leacock) Brymner would say that his parents left for Canada in 1857 when he was two years of age, and he decided to accompany them. He retained a burr, acquired from his parents, which was very pleasant. I spent many hours with him in his studio, and he was one of the few artists I knew who could go on painting and talking at the same time. He had a serious turn of mind, and having read some of the articles he contributed to a university magazine I think he could have made a considerable reputation as a writer. If it could be said that Horatio Walker was influenced by Jean François Millet, Brymner was certainly influenced by Constable. Since paintings by Canadian artists were not yet appreciated by the public, the sales of his works were limited, and he spent a great deal of time teaching. He was a great teacher. He had the art of communicating – infinite patience, and a personal appearance that was like an assurance in itself. His style or manner of painting was too set to be much influenced by the 'revolutionaries' around him, and his work takes us back to the tonalities of the nineteenth century. He was a man I was proud to call a friend, and I regretted not having better success at selling his work, nor even being able to give him a full-scale one-man show. He died abroad in 1925. Among his pupils who carried on to distinction were A.Y. Jackson, Edwin Holgate, and Clarence Gagnon who said, 'If Brymner couldn't teach you, nobody could.' Brymner was a great admirer of Maurice Cullen, and always came to his exhibitions.

We could never have survived in business solely on the sale of Canadian paintings, and so during these difficult years more than half the paintings sold were Dutch, French, and English. These I purchased on my annual trips to Europe. On one of these trips, in 1910, I bought a small but eminently representative painting by Vincent Van Gogh. I feel almost reluctant to record this – but I could not sell it in Montreal, not even to any of the established collectors. They thought it was too crude. Needing a constant flow of capital, I could not afford to hold onto it, so the next year I took it back to the dealer from whom I had bought it in Amsterdam for $750. He seemed absolutely delighted to exchange it for ten contemporary Dutch paintings. I heard afterwards that the value of Van Gogh had doubled in less than a year. You can imagine how keenly I wished I could have kept it.

In England many of my best purchases were from Hazel Vicars, senior partner in Vicars Brothers, of Bond Street, London. John Ogilvy had introduced me as 'Canada's coming art dealer.' Hazel Vicars was to me the ideal of what an art dealer could be. He was a remarkable man. In London his judgement was so highly respected that he acted as mediator whenever there was any dispute among his colleagues, thus helping them to avoid litigation. If no agreement could be reached among the London dealers over the sale of a painting, or if there were doubts about its authenticity, they would inevitably say 'We will put it up to Hazel Vicars.' He had a fundamental honesty, and keen perception.

He was a good friend as well as a colleague, and he looked for Krieghoffs and Verners for me in London, and watched for special paintings that I needed in Canada. Some of these were portraits of 'ancestors.' This was an amusing sideplay to our work from which we both had considerable fun as well as excellent profits. It was apparently one of the irrational characteristics of the 'flapper age' that followed the first world war. In the period of champagne in the slipper, there was an inexplicable American demand for 'ancestors.' It was difficult to credit the question asked by one American visitor after another who came into my gallery: 'Have you any old portraits?' I had been told about this fascination in England, before I returned to Canada after my naval service in the war (of which more later), and so I gambled by buying a few eighteenth century portraits of pretty women and distinguished-looking men. The names of the artists apparently made no difference. I spent some money on restoration, which might have included the improvement of a subject's retroussé nose, and fitting the canvases into elaborate frames, preferably of the approximate period.

No effort was required to sell these paintings. Most buyers seemed delighted to have found plausible 'ancestors.' One naval officer who found a Nelson-like admiral was particularly pleased. This incredible nonsense of inverted pride dwindled in a few years, but by that time I did not have a single 'ancestor' left. The profit from these sales often supplied the cash necessary to buy Canadian paintings. In his own gallery Hazel sold the great English masters such as Lawrence, Hogarth, Gainsborough, and Reynolds. All these paintings were beyond my reach.

Hazel reacted forcibly against all fraudulent practices, of which there were far too many in certain sections of the art world. He enjoyed the story I once told him about a painter of seascapes he knew well, whose pictures I had been buying for years. In a London auction room I saw what I considered a bad fake attributed to this man, and signed and catalogued. I took a taxi and went to the artist's studio to tell him about it. He was very angry. We immediately went back to the auction room, and as soon as he saw the painting he agreed it was a fake, signature and all. He took a pen knife out of his pocket and calmly slashed the canvas. We then went to the office together where he introduced himself by saying, 'I am not a lunatic, neither am I the painter of that bloody picture I've just cut to ribbons in its frame. Here is my card, and you can let me hear from you.' In a few days he received a letter from the auction firm, full of contrition, admitting he had done them a service, as his action was stronger than words, and would ensure greater care in the future. Hazel considered our friend's action a courageous one, and remarked that he wished he had done something like that when he was a comparatively young man and saw a fake Corot painted on English canvas.

Hazel was a civilized and refined man, much loved and long remembered by his colleagues and artist friends. I admired his joyous and positive attitude to life. He loved wine and good food. One day when I went to see him in his gallery he had just sold a painting by Gainsborough, and announced, 'I must celebrate – come to lunch.' So the two of us went down to Simpson's in the Strand, and Hazel promptly ordered a magnum of champagne. The very sight of it on the table overwhelmed me – I said, 'We can't drink all that.' 'Of course the two of us can,' said Hazel, and poured the first glass. We were there for over two hours, enjoying oysters, and beef carved on the spot, and glasses and glasses of champagne. I was sure he had gone a bit too far –

but the lunch over, he was able to walk out the very personification of dignity. 'Come on,' he said, 'let's be photographed together.' We crossed the Strand traffic by the grace of God, ascended a flight of stairs to a photographer's studio, and asked to have our picture taken standing together. *'Standing?'* asked the photographer, sizing us up. 'Yes,' said Hazel, 'standing.' The photographer then produced two iron stands, weighted heavily at the bottom, with a half-circle at the top, the kind then used in slow-exposure photography. He placed our necks in the half circles, to steady us. That old photograph is a cherished memento of one of the finest men I ever met. He had infinite patience and his kindness in taking me to see exhibitions in all parts of London, and pointing out the salient points in every significant painting, gave me confidence in buying in later years. I could almost say Hazel Vicars was my mentor in both life and art.

In 1912, after being seven years on Peel Street, south of Ste Catherine, my father became a commercial pioneer of the corner of Peel and Burnside, opening his antique store opposite some red brick buildings where the Mount Royal Hotel now stands. It was not a good move. Both our businesses languished and we realized the importance of location. Two years later we moved to very good premises on Ste Catherine, east of Bishop Street. Business was excellent there, and a large shop window on this busy street was an important attraction.

Dark clouds gathering over Europe foretold the first world war, and August 4, 1914 became a day of destiny for many. After hesitating for over a year, I joined the Royal Navy (there was then no Canadian Navy), being recruited in Montreal by a Lieutenant representing the British Admiralty. I apparently had the right qualifications to enrol at the Royal Naval College, since I owned a motor-boat and a canoe and had some knowledge of navigation. In the navy I became involved with hydrophones, and fortuitously invented a submarine direction-finder, for which I was partly rewarded by being detained for several months of post-war special service, which included testing dives with my new equipment in a miserable Class C-3 submarine. The Secretary of the Admiralty at Whitehall in London saw fit to inform my senior officer in the following manner:

I am to acquaint you that the Board have had brought to their notice the good organizing ability and zeal displayed by Lieutenant W.R. Watson, RNVR, in connection with the Hydrophone organization, and I am to request that an expression of Their Lordships' appreciation be conveyed to Lieutenant Watson, and that he may be informed that a notation of his good service has been made in his record.

This general appreciation was soon followed by a handsome award from the Admiralty (the Royal Commission on Awards to Inventors) for my invention of the Compass Bearing Finder.

I returned home to Canada from my naval service in April 1919, and again established myself in the little gallery in my father's antique shop. My father's business had continued to flourish despite the war, but one year after its end he died, and my brother and sisters were unable to carry it on. So, in 1921, with the blessing of friends in London and Paris, I opened my own exclusive art gallery at the corner of Ste Catherine and Bishop Streets, with the somewhat flamboyant title of the Watson Art Galleries. I put up the sign on the building with the boldness of a banner. I now hoped to realize the dream I had cherished since walking into John Ogilvy's gallery sixteen years before.

3
In Pursuit of Krieghoff

Mr Ogilvy had often talked about an artist 'who had lived across the river' (Longueuil), with whom he had gone on hunting expeditions between 1848 and 1850. The man had the sharp eyes of a bird and painted pictures that were like enlarged miniatures. His name was Cornelius Krieghoff. According to Mr Ogilvy, his eyesight was almost miraculous – he could see details at a distance which other hunters would have detected only with a glass. He was a great walker, loved the woods, and made trips with Indians, whose portraits he often painted. One of his best friends was a Huron chief, who was the last one to speak the language of his forefathers and who never wore a hat. Krieghoff had told Mr Ogilvy that some of his colours were based on information given him by this old chief, among them a peculiar blue, and his vermillion, which was very brilliant and preserved remarkably well. These colours were unusual and chemically different from the average commercial product of the time. His pictures, when cleaned today, for that reason have a remarkable freshness which often gives the impression of their having been painted within the last few months.

Mr Ogilvy incited my interest in Krieghoff, and when I asked where I could see some of his pictures, he kindly arranged for me to go to the house of a friend who had eight good examples. I recognized the technique as of the Dusseldorf school. The subjects were painted honestly and were essentially Canadian, with habitants, Indians, birch-bark canoes, and one *Bilking the Toll* scene that at once endeared him to me as a humourist with a light touch. I thought that being so factual, his pictures would become increasingly interesting to a generation of Canadians who had never tried to bilk a tollgate or seen Indians in their natural habitat. I told Mr Ogilvy of my interest, and suggested that we try to obtain one for sale. But where? Krieghoff had then been dead for thirty-three years and his paintings were distributed over a wide area. We never had one for sale while I was with him, although Mr Ogilvy had purchased two in the past directly from Krieghoff for about $50 each. Mr Ogilvy once mentioned that a Montreal gentleman had bought fifteen water colours in London for a song; he thought they were by Krieghoff but they turned out to be by James Duncan.

In 1908, when Mr Ogilvy took me to Europe, my own search for Krieghoffs began. In London I drifted into a rather shabby art dealer's shop, and there I found my first, which I bought for Mr Ogilvy personally at a very small price. The dealer told me it had come from an old military family in Edinburgh. The owner's grandfather was said to have brought it from Canada around 1865. This incident opened a magic door for me. The key was 'military family,' for I then deduced that the missing Krieghoffs (missing from Canada) had been brought back to England and Scotland by returning officers of the British garrison in Quebec, probably as visual souvenirs. I kept this secret to myself for more than ten years, and when later I had my own gallery, I hunted for and managed to buy over a hundred Krieghoff paintings of all sizes, subjects, and periods.

The source for some purchases was of course Christie's and Sotheby's auction rooms in London, and my art dealer friend Hazel Vicars would occasionally find some for me. Krieghoffs usually turned up in the auction room as some undistinguished part of an estate, scarcely noticed among the furniture and other household effects. I would often get people outside the trade to bid for me – thus succeeding for several years in keeping the interest in Krieghoff a mystery.

This pursuit of the 'lost' Krieghoffs reached a climax in 1913. On one of my routine prowls in London I had drifted into a Pall Mall auction room and, browsing among the so-called 'cheap stuff,' discovered five interesting paintings stacked against the wall on the floor. There were three in one bundle, and two in another, all of them tied up with string. Only junk was treated in such a way, but from only the very small sections of them I could see, I felt certain they were Krieghoffs. I dared not look too much to betray my interest, and wondered if anyone else had recognized what they were. The sale was to be the next day at 10 AM. I went to my bank and took out £300. I don't think I slept much that night.

The next morning I took a taxi to the auction rooms, and it occurred to me that I should ask the cab driver to come in and bid for me. Certainly no one would take him for an art dealer, Canadian or otherwise. He gladly agreed. I told him to keep away from me, but to watch me. He was to bid by nodding his head as long as I kept my hat on. The unimportant 'floor lots' were up for bidding first, so there was not long to wait. I was glad when the floor-man held up the first parcel of two Krieghoffs. The auctioneer said they were by 'Kree-eg-koff' or some other Russian-sounding name, and asked for a bid of 10 shillings to start. My cabby nodded his head. Nobody else was bidding seriously. They went from 10 shillings to one guinea each, and then were knocked down to my driver. 'Will the buyer take the others at the same price?' asked the auctioneer. My hat stayed on, my man nodded his head, the auctioneer banged his gavel, and they were sold. I went with my cab-man to the office, declared myself the buyer, and offered to pay cash, plus a £2 tip to the floor-man to get immediate delivery. It was over in about ten minutes, and I found myself wondering if it had all been a dream, everything seemed so utterly absurd.

But the pictures were beside me as we drove to my hotel, and I could see enough of the smaller ones to be absolutely certain that they were Krieghoffs. The cab driver seemed to have enjoyed his unusual experience, and said, 'I've never spent so much money on stuff like that in my life.' I felt slightly intoxicated, with a warm generous feeling, so I asked if he were married. 'Yes sir,' he said, 'and with three children.' When we arrived at the hotel, I said, 'You're a fine fellow, here's five pounds for yourself, and five pounds for your wife, and one pound each for the children,' and I tossed the thirteen pounds on the seat beside him. As soon as I stepped out of the cab with my two precious parcels, he roared away in second gear without even thanking me. I imagine he drove straight home and told his wife he had met a lunatic.

The paintings proved to be perfect untouched Krieghoffs of his

Quebec period, dated 1865–66. They all looked as though they had been out of their frames for years. They had cost me about $25. Like penitents who confess the same sin for years because they like talking about it, I must confess that that rare bonanza has caused me many a chuckle of pleasure. I like thinking about it. It was so much like something one only dreams of happening. I have often thought of all the fortunate people who, in the early years, bought Krieghoffs (as well as other Canadian pictures) from us, and have seen their value increase since. It is almost unbelievable.

Discovering those five Krieghoffs in an auction room in London in 1913 was fortuitous, but it did happen again, although less dramatically. Over the years I was to find in North America other fine paintings by Krieghoff, but both locating them and buying them often required great determination. As an example, one day, quite by accident, I came across a reference to Krieghoff having sold two of his best pictures 'to a gentleman of importance from Philadelphia.' I hunted down clue after clue until at last I discovered that they were in the collection of the Pennsylvania Museum of Art in Philadelphia, but were not actually on view. I have kept the letters which tell the subsequent story of two of the finest of his paintings we ever had. It is to be noted that it took patience and persistence and finally, after eleven years, a touch of sentiment, to bring the paintings back to Canada.

In early 1934, I wrote to the Pennsylvania Museum of Art enquiring about the pictures, and received this reply:

> We do have in the Wilstach Collection at this Museum two paintings by Cornelius Krieghoff, one 'Canadian Winter Scenery,' dated 1857, measurements 24″ x 36″. The other a Landscape, measurements 16″ x 24″. These are in storage at the Museum at the present time. If I can do anything further for you I will be glad to do so.

I wrote again, asking if we could purchase the paintings, and was informed that they were controlled by the executors of the Wilstach Estate. I persisted, asking if we could perhaps make an exchange. In June 1934 my correspondent replied:

> I am afraid the ruling of the Commissioners of Fairmount Park, which control

the Wilstach Collection, is final, and that the pictures can neither be sold or exchanged.

I have done my best, and I am afraid we have to abandon the hope of further progress.

Years passed. Quite by chance, in 1945 I saw a notice in an American publication referring to the Wilstach Estate. I wrote again, asking if now the two Krieghoff paintings could be returned to their native land. To my delight, I received the following:

I am happy to say the Commissioners of Fairmount Park accept your offer of May 29 for the two Krieghoffs, and I enclose their bill.

Pending receipt of your draft and the necessary invoices we shall be packing the two paintings, for immediate dispatch.

I am glad the matter is happily concluded, as it was only made possible by changes in the personnel of the Commission since our first correspondence years ago.

There was much excitement in our Gallery when the crate from Philadelphia was opened. The two beautiful Krieghoffs were in perfect condition, and as clean as if they had been kept in a glass case all those years. We celebrated with champagne.

As recently as 1956, when I enquired about the provenance of two other Krieghoffs we had just purchased, I received the following frank and revealing letter, this time from western Ontario.

This will confirm our telephone conversation of to-day's date in which I accepted your offer of $4500.00 (Forty-five hundred dollars) for the two pictures by Krieghoff namely 'A Winter Scene' and 'Habitants going to Market.'

As to their history, there is little I can tell you. The first I heard of them was on my son's return from the Coronation in 1937. He had seen them on my sister's wall in East Malling, Kent, England and had remarked about them. It seems that my brother-in-law had been at an auction somewhere near Maidstone, Kent and had bought a hamper of bric a brac and odds and ends. He paid 10/- sight unseen and found the pictures in the hamper.

When my son was again in England with the army, he wrote in 1943 to the

National Gallery, Ottawa, for information about Krieghoff but the Director was very noncommittal about the pictures until he could see them or a photograph of them. Because of the difficulty of getting photographs during the war, he was not able to proceed any further.

My sister died in 1952 and I obtained the two pictures. Because of British Government red tape, Board of Trade export permits, currency control, etc., it was 1953 before I was able to get their delivery here in Fort Frances.

I had been in correspondence with the National Gallery and sent them the pictures for inspection. I don't suppose anything had been done in the way of cleaning the paint since they were painted. The Gallery did what restoration was necessary, cleaned and varnished them and replaced keys in the stretchers.

This is all I can tell you and unfortunately there is no way of finding out the exact location of the house from which they originally came so as to learn how they found their way from Canada to England. We surmise that they must have been picked up in Quebec or Montreal by a member of the British garrison and taken home when his tour of duty was completed. Now at last they have made the circle and returned from whence they came.

I hope that this purchase will prove profitable to you. It has been a pleasure to do business with you.

This is probably one of the most honest, yet bizarre instances of hidden treasure so casually obtained. The sequel is that these two paintings fetched a very high price when sold at auction in Toronto in 1969.

I still believe in the dramatic or fortuitous discovery of more fine Krieghoffs. The search need never end. This gives an idea what a fascinating profession an art dealer's is. It is like endless exploration and discovery. But acquisitions likely will never again be as easy as they once were. After one or two great Krieghoff exhibitions, the market for his paintings became keenly competitive, and my own particular secret became a plume of smoke.

Looking over my records of over forty years of exhibitions of contemporary Canadian art, of the French paintings bought in Paris, and the Dutch paintings in Amsterdam, I am still surprised at what a wide range of splendid Kreighoffs I actually managed to bring back to Canada.

I am also amazed at the increasing value of his work. For example, Lord Beaverbrook paid $25,000 for *The Merry Makers* in 1959, and a smaller picture called *Indians Camping at Big Rock* sold at a Christie's auction in Montreal in 1969 for $36,000. I can make no comment without disturbing Krieghoff's ghost, for I have seen £20 as the price he marked on the backs of equally good canvases, and he sold some for as low as £5.

When Mr Ogilvy told me what he knew about Krieghoff, I made some notes of the conversations, and nearly thirty years later I mentioned this to my friend Marius Barbeau, who was writing a book on Krieghoff and was glad to have any authentic information he could get. Barbeau's enthusiasm was infectious and together we made several visits to Longueuil, across the river from Montreal where Krieghoff had lived in 1841. We drove into the surrounding country in the hope of finding some relative of the Gautier family (his wife's surname), or even an identifiable house which could have been his home. We thought we had found the house of *The Horse Trader* painting, but Krieghoff had a way of transposing things for art's sake, so we were never really certain. If we could have found a few words of correspondence to say that he was changing his house or living in a particular place, we might have had something tangible to go on. But we both enjoyed being in 'Krieghoff territory' as it were, and we saw his ghost everywhere.

Barbeau's book was the work of a scholar, and required a great deal of research. He was tireless in tracking down the smallest bit of interesting information. A.Y. Jackson told us that his grandfather saw Krieghoff in Longueuil quite frequently, and that he had actually bought three paintings from him there.

As part of my own study of Krieghoff, I found and photographed eight extremely varied signatures, which Barbeau included in his book, published in 1934. Unfortunately these photographs simplified the work of forgers. Over the years I have seen paintings by Joseph Dynes (1825–1897), James Duncan (1806–1880), and Coke Smyth (after 1840), with the names carefully changed to 'C. Krieghoff,' and sometimes even dated. It is a pity that forgeries and fakes have been increasing in the last few years, almost in proportion to the increase in value of good Canadian paintings. Krieghoff has been subject to these fraudulent practices more than any other artist.

4
Maurice Cullen

Of all the artists I came to know, none was closer to me than Maurice Cullen. My first impression on meeting him around 1908 was of an uncommon personality. He was physically of medium height, broad shouldered and muscular, with a ruddy complexion that told of a life spent largely outdoors. His quiet poise and manner of speech, his calm contemplative blue-grey eyes, revealed a deep spiritual quality, the inner peace of a man in harmony with his environment and the world. He was then thirty-eight years of age and to me he seemed to have somehow solved all of life's problems.

Questioning his philosophy of life, I found it very much akin to that of Emerson or Thoreau, especially in his love of nature. I think I would describe him as a transcendental-pantheist; he would often admit to me how profound and all-embracing this love of nature was. 'One justification for living,' he would say, 'is the understanding and love of beauty.' Perhaps, however, I came to understand him even better through his art.

On the advice of the Montreal sculptor, Philippe Hébert, Maurice Cullen had gone to Paris in 1889 to study sculpture. He entered the École des Beaux Arts, but had not been there long before he realized that his real vocation was painting and exchanged his chisel for a brush. About three years later he left the Beaux Arts and began to paint landscapes, working entirely outdoors, and became fascinated by the Impressionist painters, notably Monet and Sisley.

Five years after his arrival in France, the French Government purchased his first winter landscape, which was painted in Brittany, and he was elected an Associate of the Societé des Beaux Arts, a distinct honour, for the membership included Degas, Rodin, Whistler, and Forain. He immediately received a few commissions. This success tempted him to remain in France, but fortunately for us, a nostalgic yearning for Canada brought about his return in 1895. This date marked a new epoch in Canadian painting, for Cullen had studied the clean palette of the Impressionists, and let daylight into the Canadian landscape. He was the father of modern Canadian painting, for not until then had any hint appeared of development beyond Constable or the Barbizon School. Canadian art was academic and derivative. Paul Kane, Cornelius Krieghoff, and Otto Jacobi were studio painters in the broadest sense, and although they occasionally sketched outdoors, the results were hardly to be distinguished from the work done in their studios.

Cullen was considered a revolutionary by his Canadian contemporaries, and indeed he was. His broad, bold compositions, his scorn for irrelevant details, and his robust colour, were rather disturbing to the maulstick painters of his day. The younger artists, such as Clarence Gagnon and Albert Robinson, were stimulated and influenced by him and A.Y. Jackson has called him 'our hero.'

James Wilson Morrice, who was living in Paris, clearly recognized Cullen's significance as the pioneer of modern Canadian art and wrote to a friend in 1910:

> Healthy, lusty colour which you see in Canada is no doubt considered vulgar – Cullen, I see by the papers, has painted a good picture – he is the man in Canada who gets at the guts of things.

From time to time when Morrice came to Canada, he and Cullen painted together at Beaupré. For the perceptive lover of Morrice's work, this was the brief period when he painted with a more fully loaded brush and a light impasto, such as Cullen always had. Both were showing us the beauty and character of our winter.

Cullen not only 'got at the guts of things,' but the soul of them as well. He was mentally and physically robust, and loved to tramp on snowshoes to the northern woods for his subjects. He said 'nature was a book, with most of the leaves still uncut.' He gloried in the Laurentians, and to become familiar with the mountains he built himself a shack at the edge of Lac Tremblant where he lived and worked alone for over three months at a time. Here he painted some of his finest works, and through them revealed a new and authentic Canadian expression. He experimented with the light colours of the Impressionists and achieved the creation of atmosphere without loss of form. He did not try to paint in broken tones, for the rugged Canadian landscape itself influenced his technique. The powerful rhythmic lines of mountains, the strong darks of spruce and pine, and the lusty colour, could hardly be painted in the style of Monet. Here was landscape that inspired bold and vigorous composition, and Cullen evolved a synthesis of design based on the truths of nature rather than the inventions of the mind. 'When pattern becomes the main thing,' said Cullen, 'I shall begin to design rugs.'

During his early years in Montreal, he painted city streets, preferably in winter, and on at least one occasion in a swirling blizzard. Quite often he painted ice-cutters at work on the St Lawrence River, but the lonely Laurentians were always his greatest love. I went with him on occasion to those districts where the Devil, North, and Caché rivers cut through the landscape, Cullen plodding with his short tireless steps on snowshoes, and myself exhausted on my first pair of huge Norwegian skis. I have watched him work in temperatures when the paint seemed difficult to manipulate. These were the first fresh panels from which larger paintings were done in the studio, and which were sometimes transformed into his magnificent pastels. These sketches are complete works of art in themselves. Cullen was never a drawing-room painter of snow, but, tramping out from his isolated shack into the wintry weather, which he described as comfortable and bracing to work in, he met his landscapes zestfully face to face. For every finished picture he painted an original outdoor sketch, and even on occasion he would take an entire canvas with him into the snowy landscape to complete it on the spot. One of these magnificent canvases, *Levis from Quebec*, is in the collection of the Art Gallery of Ontario. He never minded miles of tramping through the snow with sketch box, canvas, and easel, freezing fingers, stiffened paints, and other physical discomforts that would

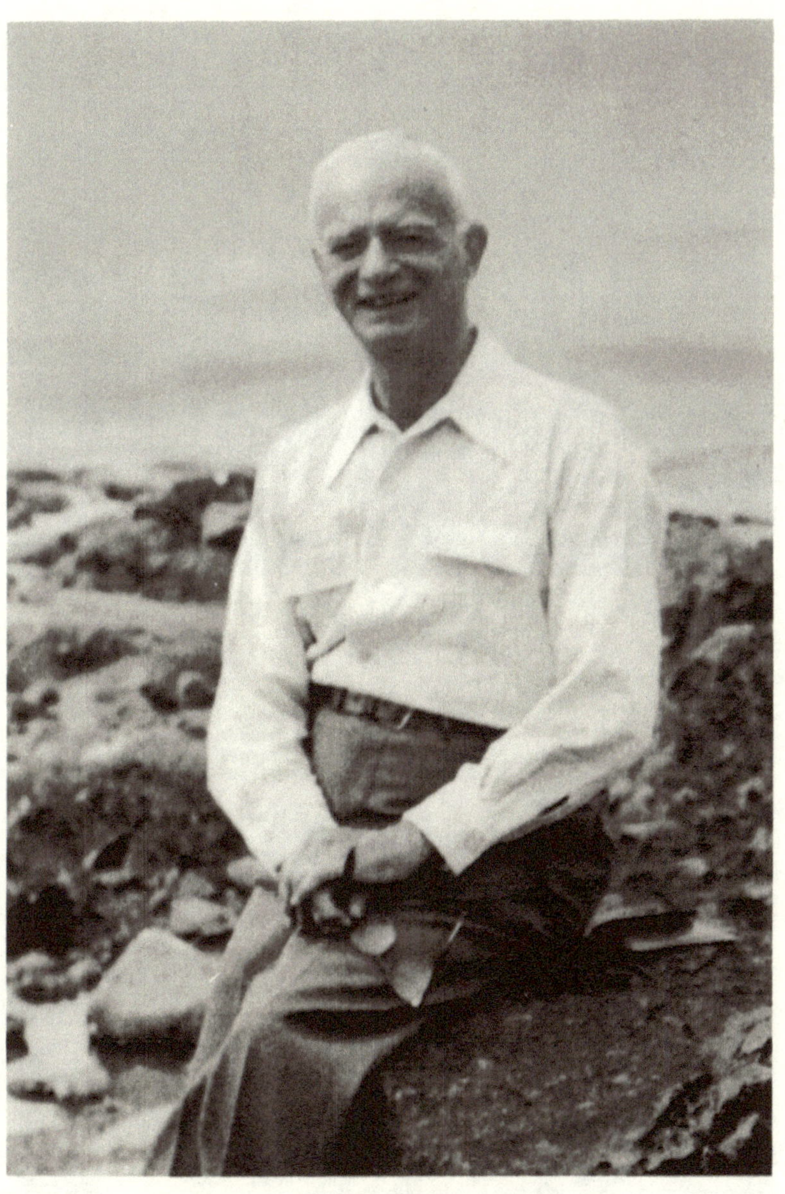

The author

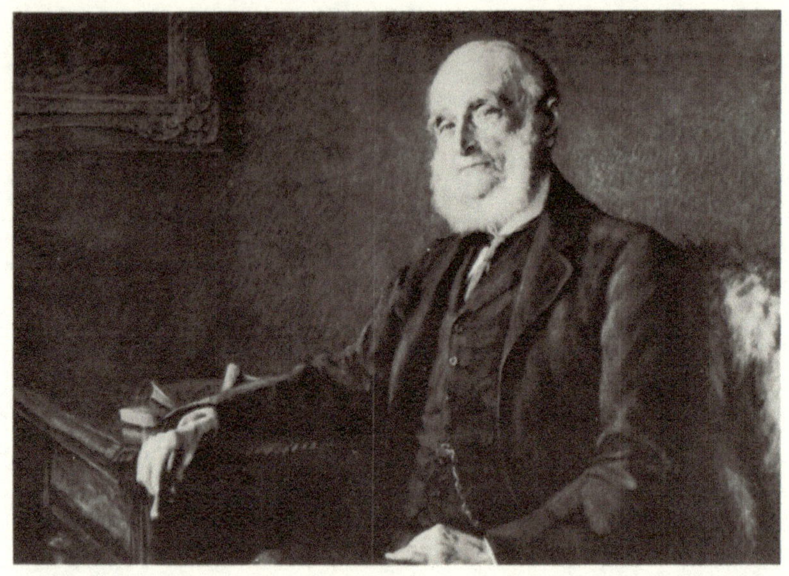

John Ogilvy (1825–1923). Water colour by L.M. Kilpin *Courtesy of St James's Club*

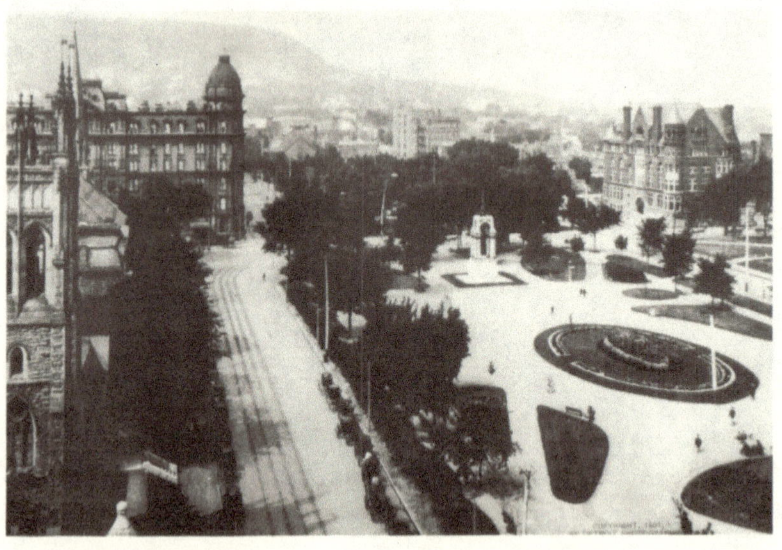

Dominion Square, Montreal, in 1905 *Sun Life Archives*

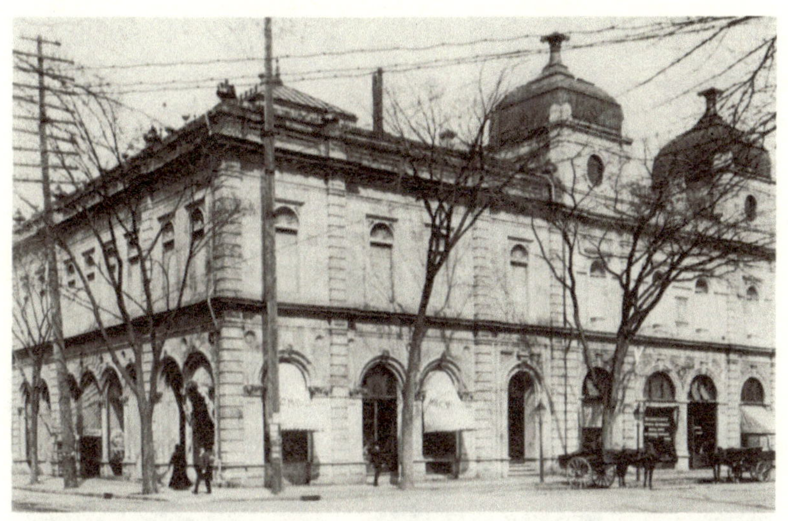

The Art Association of Montreal, Canada's first art gallery, on Phillips Square in 1910 *Notman Photographic Archives, McCord Museum of McGill University*

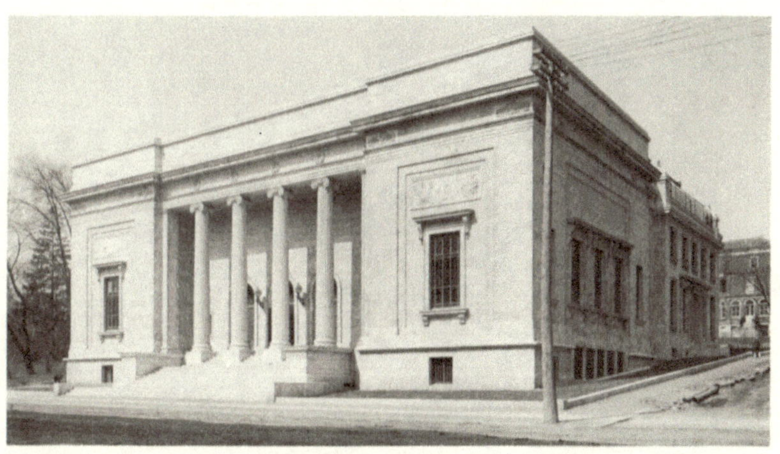

The Art Association's new building (now the Montreal Museum of Fine Arts) in 1913, soon after its opening and before Sherbrooke Street in front of it was paved *Notman Photographic Archives, McCord Museum of McGill University*

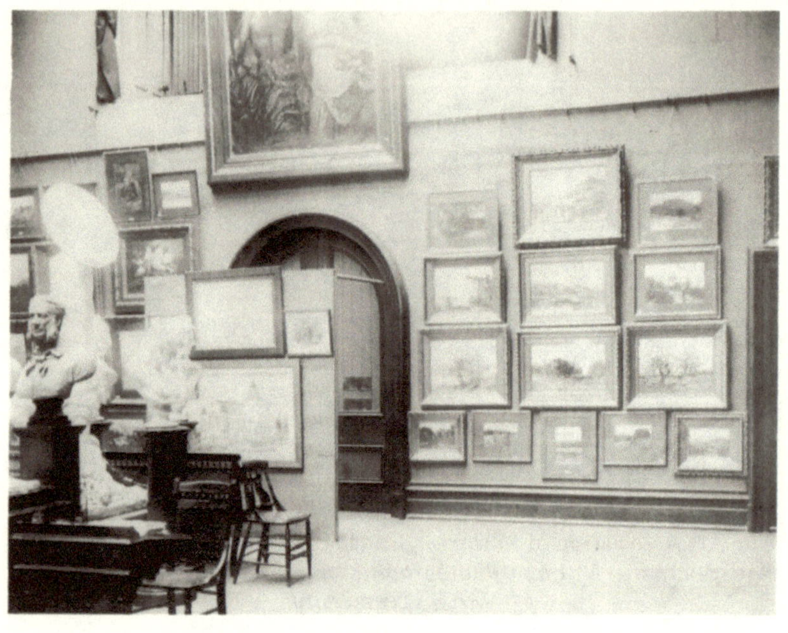

The National Gallery of Canada, 1908

James W. Morrice, RCA (1865–1924)

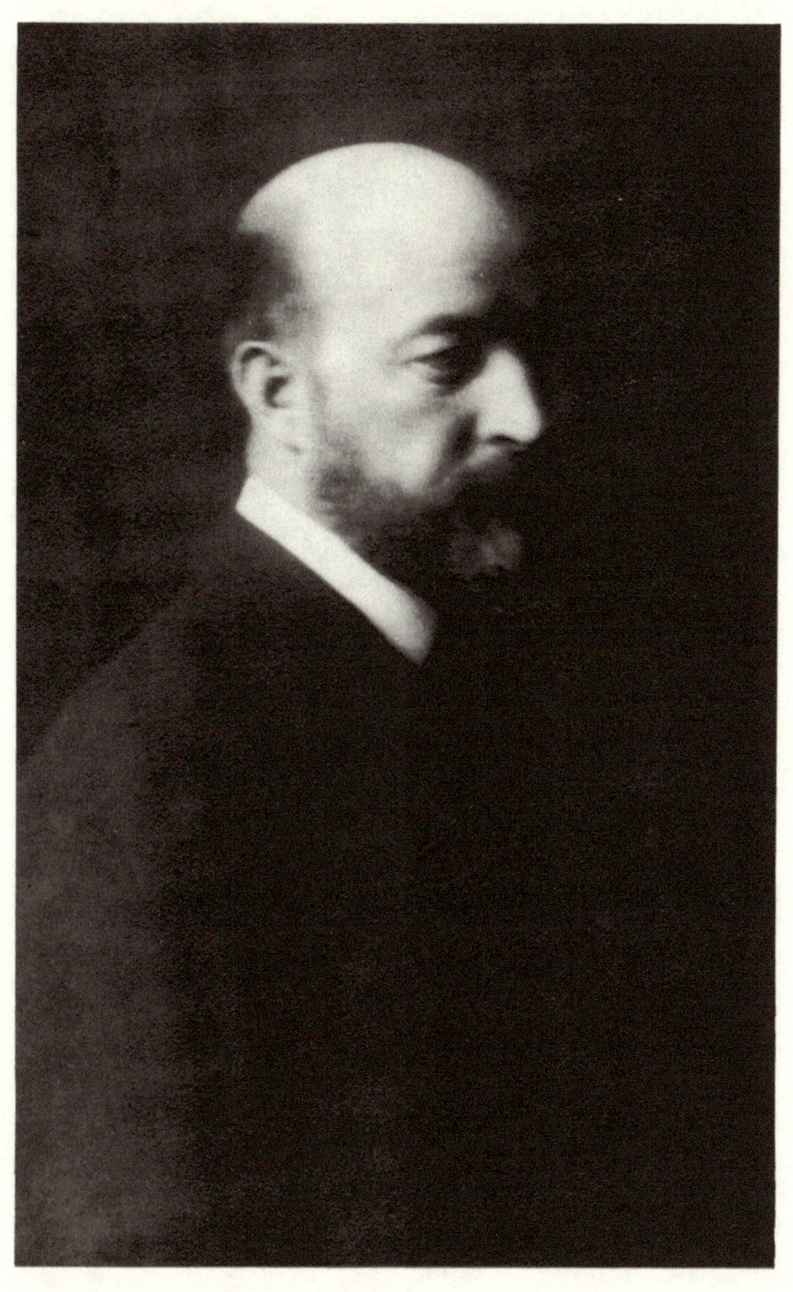

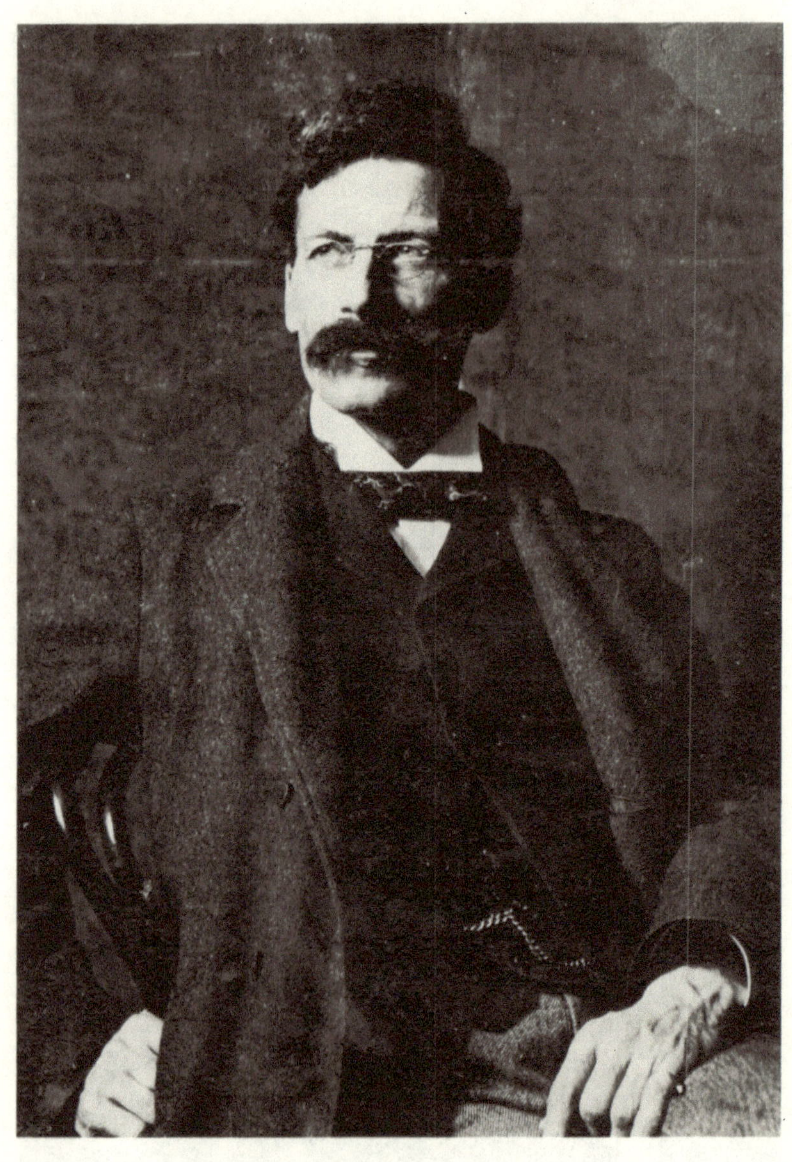

William Brymner, RCA (1855–1925)

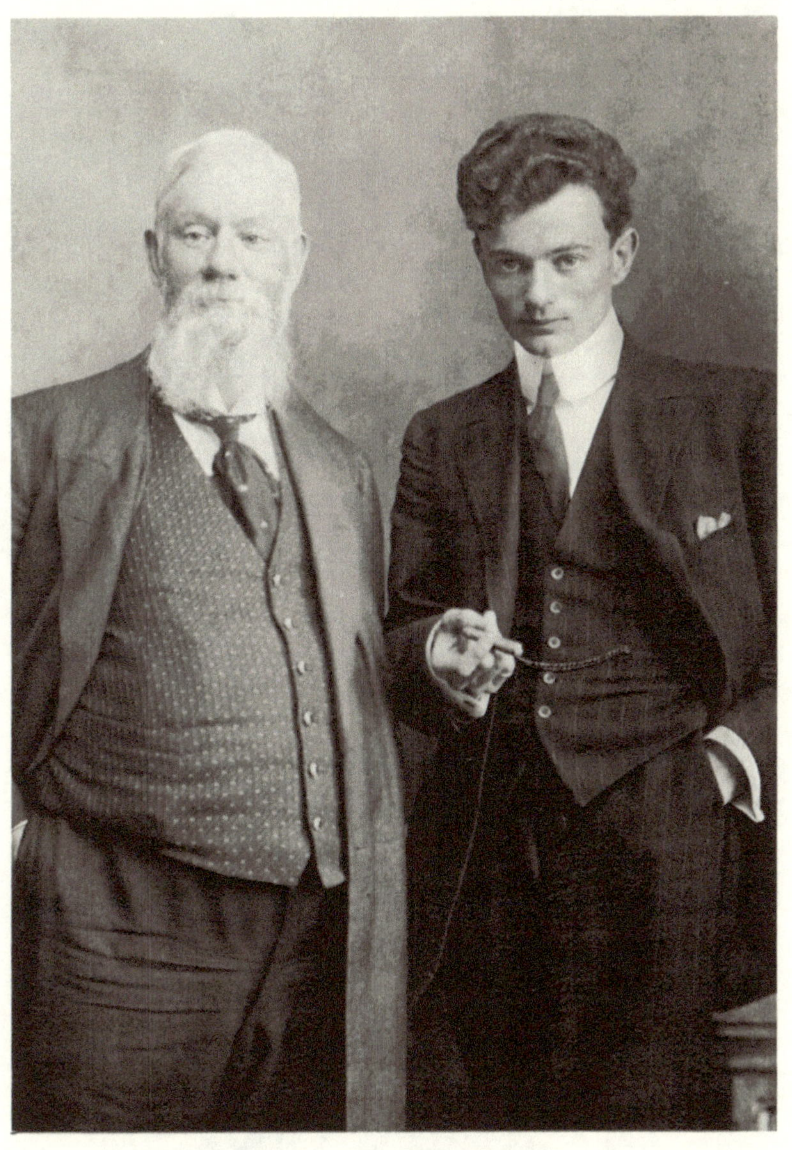

Hazel Vicars and the author in London, 1912

Maurice Cullen, RCA (1866–1934)

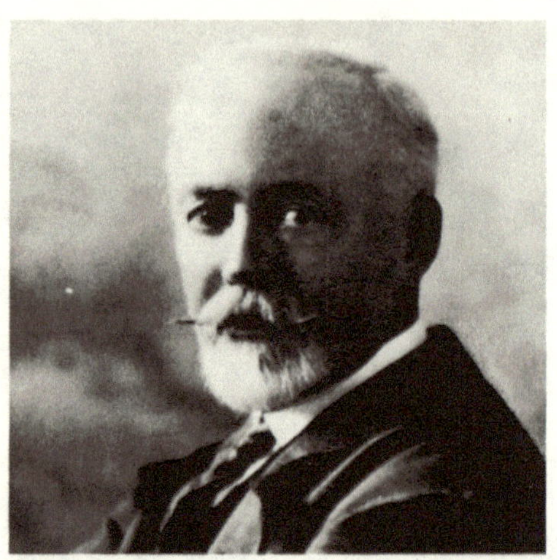

Cullen, sketching near St Jovite, Quebec, in 1925

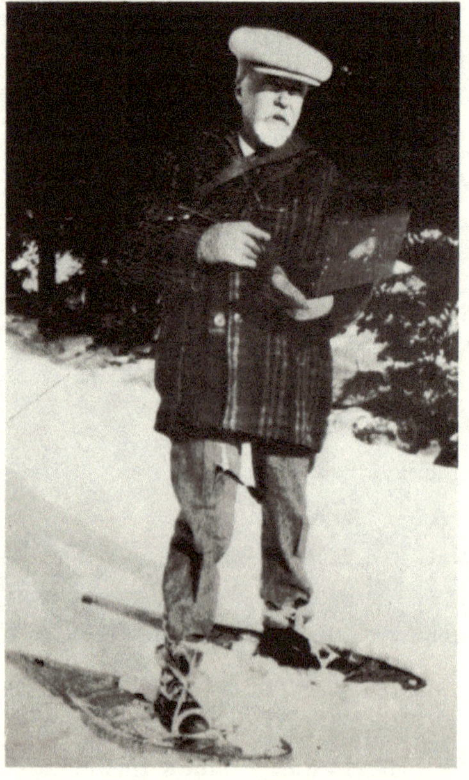

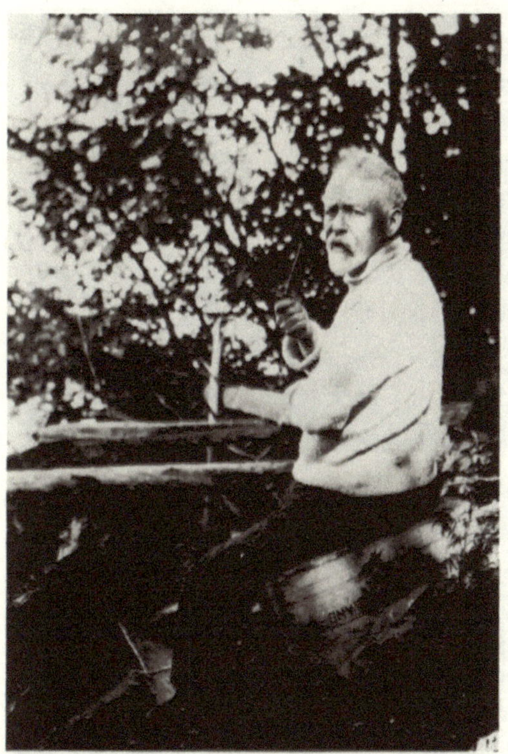

Cullen
in his garden
at Chambly, Quebec,
1930

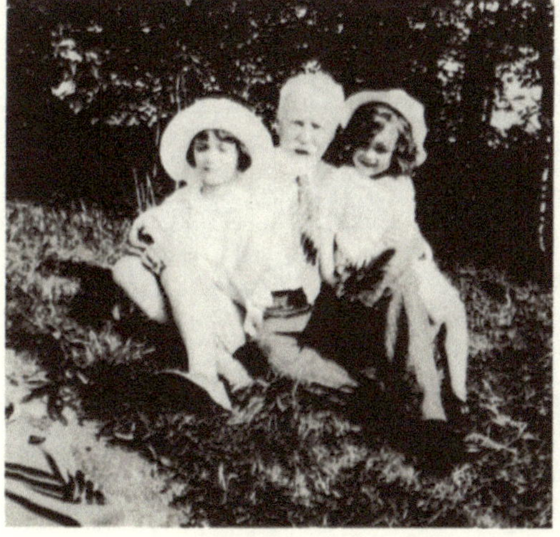

Cullen
with the author's
daughters

Clarence Gagnon, RCA (1881–1942)

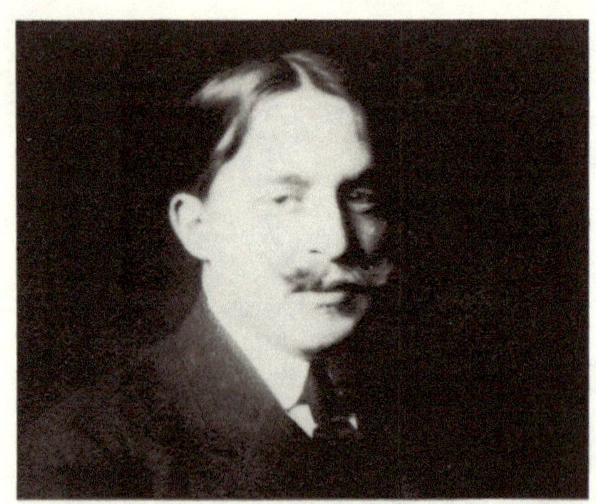

Robert Pilot, RCA (1897–1967)

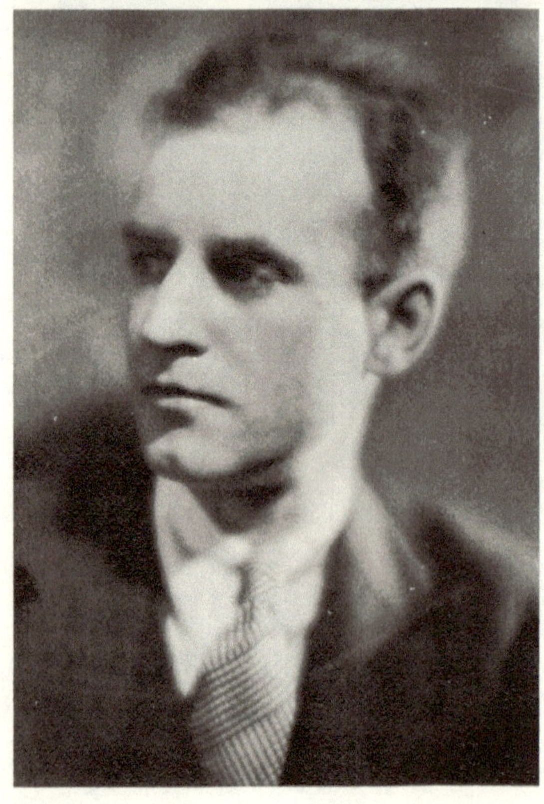

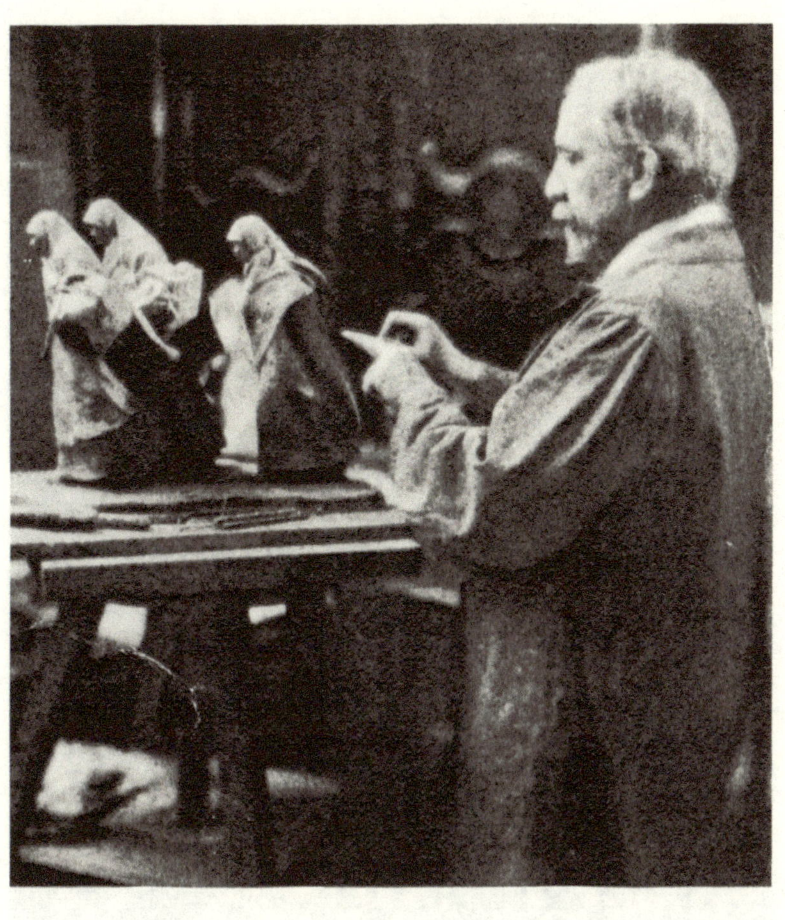

M.A. Suzor Côté, RCA (1869–1937)
with his bronze, *Three Indian Women*

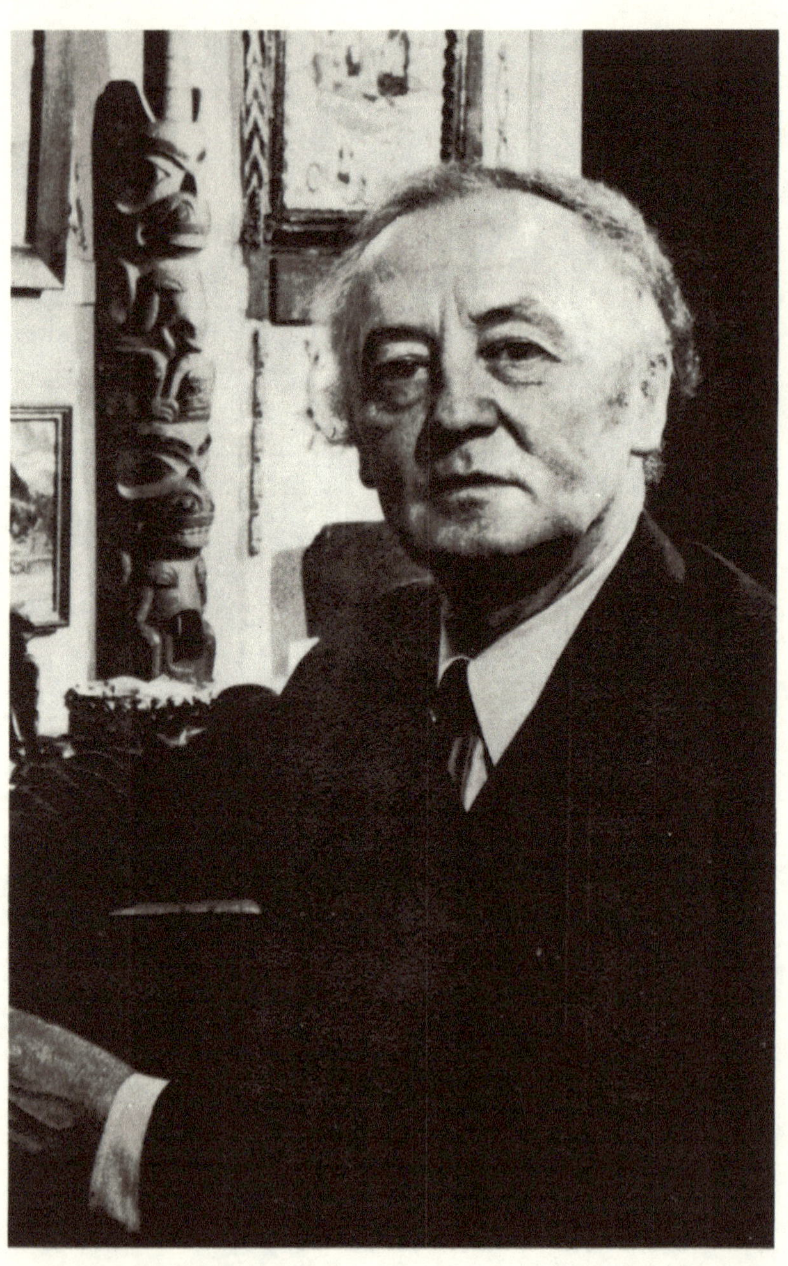

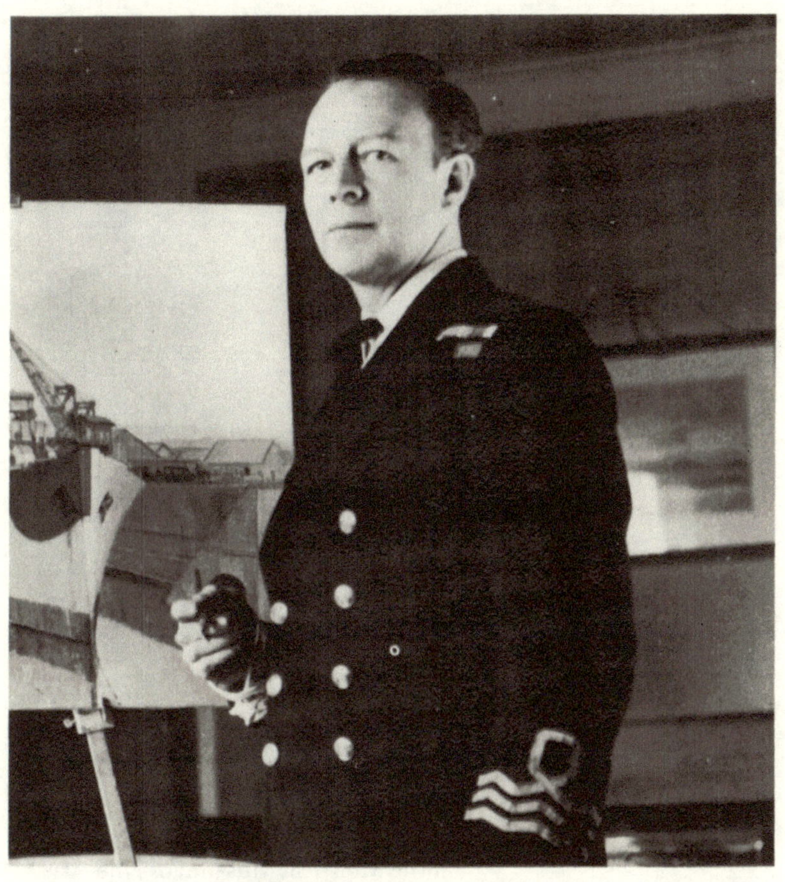

Harold Beament, RCA (1898–   )

Marius Barbeau (1883–1969)

F.W. Hutchison, NA, RCA (1871–1953)

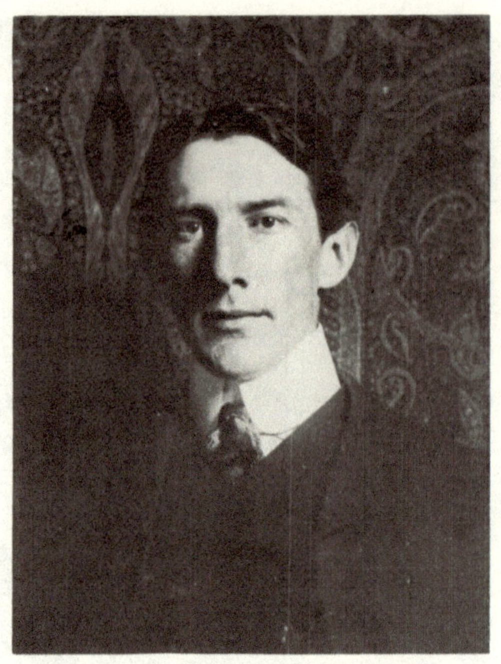

Arthur Lismer, RCA (1885–1969) in one of his art classes for children at the Montreal Museum of Fine Arts
Montreal Star-Canada Wide

John Lyman, RCA (1886–1967)
Photo by André G. de Tonnancour

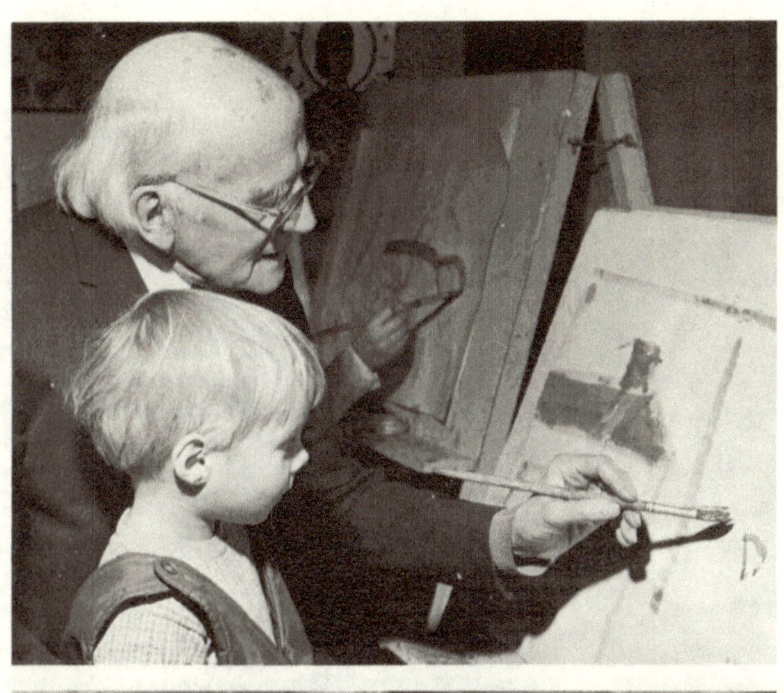

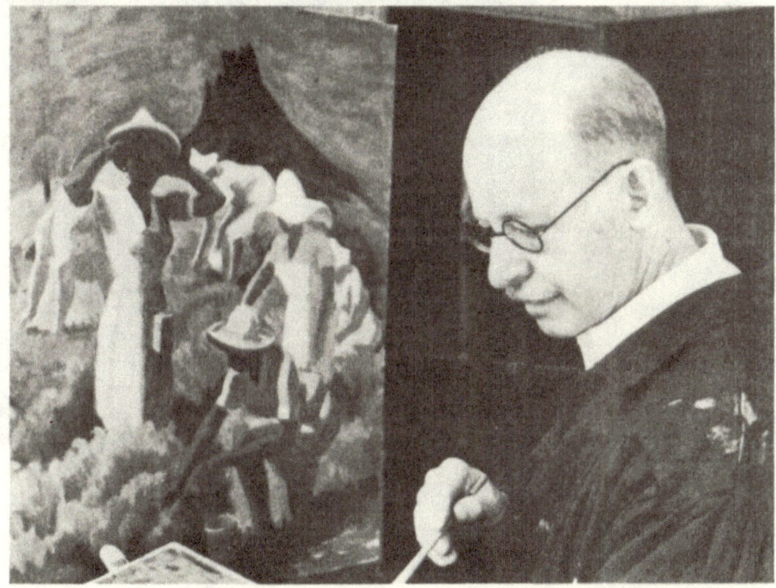

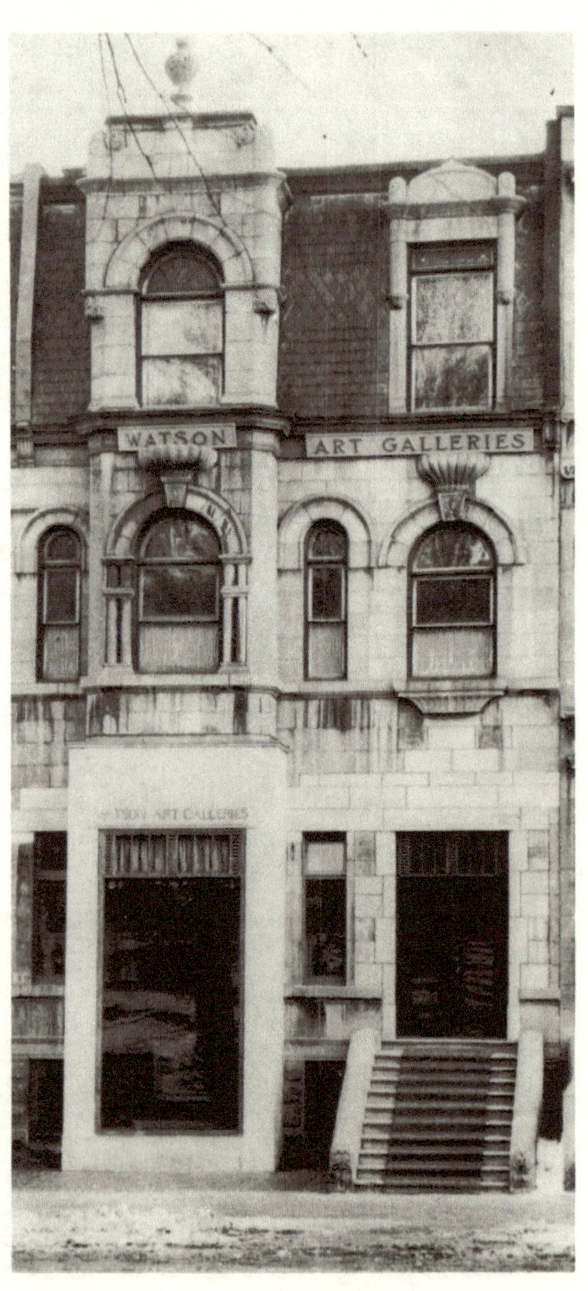

The Watson Art Galleries, 1434 Sherbrooke Street West, Montreal, 1950

have daunted many a man of less endurance and will. What could have been his inspiration other than what Conrad has called 'the obscure inner necessity to create'?

Shortly after his success in France and his return to Canada, Cullen was elected an Associate of the Royal Canadian Academy, and in 1907 he became a full member. In 1908 the National Gallery of Canada purchased one of his paintings, *First Snow*. A.Y. Jackson said that he influenced the Group of Seven more than Morrice did, and Albert Robinson said of himself that when he was discouraged, he would go to Cullen's studio and come away inspired.

It now seems difficult to believe that for almost twenty years there was little public encouragement for Cullen, and for most of his work the only reward was the joy of accomplishment. Most people were almost indifferent to Canadian art, and especially to paintings of the northern winter. Occasionally, between 1908 and 1922, I would find a discriminating buyer, among them Herbert Marler, Dr William Gardner, and Sir William Van Horne. Somehow Cullen was able to survive, as he used to say, 'just one step ahead of the wolf.' He steadily refused offers of commercial work, so tempting at that time. For him there could be no alternative but to be free to interpret the beauty of the land he loved so well. So, despite the difficulties, he continued to paint to the satisfaction of his own spirit.

His painting of the Canadian landscape was interrupted in 1918 when he was commissioned in the army as a war artist and went overseas to paint scenes of the Western Front. A brave and courageous man, he went as close as possible to the front lines to gather material for his pictures. One of these, *Dead Horse and Rider*, is a haunting interpretation of war as he saw it – a sensitive portrayal of battlefield agonies.

With his regal bearing and full beard, Cullen in uniform was frequently taken to be a top ranking officer, and he was referred to as 'General' by most of the soldiers that knew him. I liked this story, and 'General' became my own affectionate name for him. He in turn called me 'Admiral' because of my wartime service in the navy, and we used these names as our fond address for each other during the many years of our friendship.

He painted very slowly, and I would have to put paintings aside, collecting them for a year, to have enough to make an exhibition. Cullen disliked the ornate, solid frames which were seen on European paintings at that time, and began to carve his own out of chestnut wood. They were very simple and elegant. I finally persuaded him to stop doing this, as it seemed he was spending as much time on the frames as on some of his paintings. I soon found a wood-worker to make the frames to his specifications. In this way we were able to collect enough paintings for his first, and extraordinarily successful, exhibition in 1922.

Although we had sold his paintings since 1908, this was the first time we had been able to arrange a comprehensive show. For economy there was little publicity, mostly invitation cards mailed to our customers. Cullen, who doubted the success of a winter exhibition, was the most astonished man in Montreal when in two weeks we made sales that amounted to over $7,000 – at a time when money was far more valuable than it is today.

From then on, January became Cullen's 'month' and for the next decade we staged an annual exhibition of his work. At one famous exhibition in January 1929, all twenty-two paintings and pastels were sold before noon on the opening day, and all but four were *snow* scenes. So fashions changed. We came to have a waiting list of customers eager to purchase his works, and once a representative of a New York firm sought to buy the entire exhibition. Cullen refused that offer: he wanted his works to go into the homes of Canadians. Even in the depression, in January 1931, sixteen of his pictures and sketches sold for a total of more than $8,000.

Most artists were delighted to have nothing to do with the selling of their pictures, and Cullen was notoriously shy about quoting prices to anyone who visited his studio. He would tell delightful stories about crows and kingbirds, or talk about his lovely garden, and the visitors would invariably leave empty-handed. We agreed to take every picture he painted. He said, 'Let us make an agreement on that,' and we simply shook hands.

As each Cullen exhibition ended, I would feel a painful sense of loss, and would attempt to recreate the aura or mood that had haunted me for the preceding days. For consolation I would go over the photographs, but they were a far-off echo of the originals. Sometimes, however, parting with the paintings brought happy thoughts. Once, I recall, Herbert Marler, who had been appointed Canadian Minister to Japan, bought three of Cullen's best pictures to take with him, and wrote afterwards that Japanese artists and art lovers were admiring them greatly.

Cullen, to me, was doing for Canada with his painting what Sibelius did for Finland with his music. This seemed especially evident when one viewed one of the comprehensive exhibitions of his work. The first impression was how much alike his pictures seemed, but then it soon became apparent how completely different they were in mood and interpretation. Some suggested an abstraction such as silence, others a feeling of loneliness, for Cullen seldom put a figure in his landscapes, leaving everything to nature and to the viewer. There was always beauty, and that wonderful transmutation, the definition of true art, that had so impressed me in my youth.

Cullen insisted that light was one of the subjects to be painted, and this being so, he must go outdoors to paint. This suited him exactly; I often thought those snowshoes in his studio were a symbol of his love for the Laurentians which, before the days of good roads and automobiles, remained wild and comparatively lonely. He was unique and alone, an individualist by temperament. There are members of the Group of Seven whose paintings are sometimes difficult to distinguish one from another, but not so Cullen's. He had imitators but no followers. Like no other Canadian artist I knew, his art was the man. He is perhaps the greatest and the most individual landscape painter Canada has produced.

From the first of our exhibitions, Cullen was acclaimed by the critics, who wrote encouraging reviews of his work. The *Gazette* of 1928 had this to say:

> Many are the fortunate art lovers who have carried the glory of northern scenery, at varying seasons, to their homes – canvases that will give constant delight to themselves and their friends.
>
> One important work, however, is going where the general public can revel in the loveliness, the painting entitled 'Hoar Frost and Snow.' This oil has been acquired by the Art Association of Montreal and will distinctly strengthen the Canadian section at the Art Gallery.

And the *Montreal Star* reported:

> [Maurice Cullen] has gone his way year after year, studying, experimenting, building up, making progress until today he must be acclaimed one of our foremost artists and the principal interpreter of our Canadian winter, not only to outsiders, but also to ourselves.
>
> His range, however, does not exclude other seasons. He can visualise, with a vivid beauty that clings, the glorious riot of rich warm hues the autumn woodlands hold. And there has gradually grown into his art an authority, compact of long years of evolution, that commands respect. He seems to have a perfect comprehension of nature in her lonelier and more austere moods, and he enables us to identify new beauties in the texture of snow upon a meadow, of sunlight upon sodden ice, of the grey light of a winter day drawing to its close upon chilled pines and snow-clad hillsides. It is a privilege to see these pictures and the exhibition at the Watson Art Galleries has attracted an unusually large number of people. What is better still, Canadian art lovers are much more practical in their recognition of the merits of our own artists than they used to be.

Cullen was now able to fulfil his dream and material ambition 'to have a studio of my own, a shack in the mountains, an acre for a garden and every winter heavy with snow.' He could live and work in ideal surroundings at Chambly, by the Richelieu River, where the sound of rapids was like a lullaby. His studio was perfect, a stone building with a special north light window. There my wife, our two little girls, and I often visited him and his charming wife, Barbara; and his step-son Bob Pilot often joined us. These are happy memories.

It is probably in his paintings of the Laurentians that Cullen achieved his greatest power. His art is an epic to the peculiar beauty of the mountains, which winter, with such deft obliteration of detail, so wonderfully reveals. It is said that Turner discovered sunsets for Englishmen, but Cullen certainly discovered the Laurentians for us. His revelations were based on understanding and enthusiasm, for he assimilated the spirit of those characteristic rounded, glacially eroded forms. His technique holds the power of expressing the bulk and weight, so that one is aware of immense solidarity and three dimensions. His trees not merely touch the surface of the earth, they are deep-rooted in the soil. Spruce, with their stalwart vertical strength, were his favourites. Sometimes a leaning birch is introduced with its swift diagonal across the canvas – a certain characteristic of the country as well as a compositional line. Cullen also made a long and special study of ice formation and ice colour, as seen in varied lights and conditions. There is the steel-blue of mid-winter ice, viridian, jade, and even the golden-amber of flooded ice along the edge of mountain streams. In the painting of these subtle variations, Cullen may be seen as a consummate colourist. Autumn is certainly a test for the gamut and richness of an artist's palette; but his autumn landscapes were for me not always as convincing as his paintings of the snow, probably because of his preference for winter's beauty.

With his usual reverence in the face of nature, Cullen would become excessively modest. In a letter from 'La Conception,' where he had gone to paint some autumn landscapes, he wrote: 'I am getting a few sketches which may prove useful, but before the maple fall dress, I feel pretty weak, and it seems impossible to paint.' When he returned, he produced *Autumn Gold*, now in a private collection, and there has probably never been a better autumn landscape painted in Canada.

Cullen remained frankly of his country, time, and age. His work is a result of European training modified by environment and given a distinctly national flavour. His compositional lines have a classic restraint, yet his loaded, well-nourished brush stroke has, at times, the energy and fury of Van Gogh. In his running streams and tumbling waters of the spring break-up, where a smooth apron of water flows over the rapids, the technical handling echoes the excitement of the scene. Cullen loved the joyous flashes of sunlight, the glow of snow, the gleam of ice, the tumult of the freed river in the springtime, and he set down his impressions with an infectious gusto. He taught us to see beauty where we had only thought of cold.

Cullen caught with remarkable fidelity the colour of the landscapes of Quebec, just as in his earlier works he depicted the atmosphere of Montreal. An old horse and sleigh, standing forlorn under a winter's arc lamp, a group of old houses on a dingy street, or a team of horses bending to their load in a blizzard, can become memorable when invested with the revelation of the beauty to be found in the most ordinary things. This is the artist's mission in the world, and half the message of all art. Beauty of character is not confined to a limited sphere of scenes or forms, but is almost universal, and can be made manifest even to dull eyes by art's strange alchemy.

Cullen found interest in many directions and consequently many things to paint: French-Canadian farmhouses, whose sturdy architecture is almost indigenous to the province; wood-schooners under sail down the Gulf of the St Lawrence or ashore on the sands loading timber; harbour scenes with shipping and the serrated silhouette of massive grain elevators; ice-cutters with their teams crowding the ice; a primitive ox-cart bringing in a load; the Citadel of Quebec, in summer and winter; and, for one brief visit, in 1931, the Rocky Mountains. Here his knowledge of the Laurentians made him feel on more or less familiar ground, and although the sense of height eluded him in some of his canvases, the sense of bulk and weight did not.

While oils were the vehicle for the majority of his pictures, Cullen often confessed his pleasure in the flexibility of pastels. He explored the wide subtleties of tone attainable only in this medium, as seen in many of his most beautiful Laurentian scenes. Technically his treatment of pastels is highly interesting. Pastel in its crudest form is a very old medium, and one of the most permanent, as palaeolithic cave drawings testify. With some chemical knowledge, Cullen made most of his own colours from earths and other pigments which he blended to achieve the most subtle tones. At work in his studio, with pastels spread across a twelve-foot table, he gave the impression of a scientist working in a laboratory. He used as wide a range of individual tones as possible, to avoid mixing the colours on the paper itself. Thus he avoided the 'dragged' and 'chalky' effect which is often one of the drawbacks of this medium.

Cullen was one of the friends who made my profession as fascinating and rewarding as I had originally imagined it would be. When he died in 1934 I wrote a column for the Montreal *Gazette*, an appreciation and a tribute to a great man and a true friend.

'In the death of Maurice Cullen, Canada has lost one of her noblest gentlemen, and the world of art a genius whose influence is yet to be measured. His attitude in his last long sickness was as true to the character of the man as his whole life. In circumstances to try the soul of any man, he scarcely uttered a word of complaint, his concern being more for the welfare of others than for himself. Walter Savage Landor's beautiful lines seem singularly appropriate for his passing:

> Nature I've loved, and next to nature, art;
> I warmed both hands before the fire of life;
> It sinks – and I am ready to depart.

'In the long seige of ill-health, Cullen never lost his sense of humour, which was of the dry quiet kind, and always kindly in intent. He made friends by the sheer charm of his personality, even as a patient in the hospital. Not so long ago I had taken him a photograph of one of his last great pictures of the Caché, and held it before him for a few moments. He looked at it with reminiscent eyes, and said, very quietly, "Perhaps I shall bring fame to one little river." Such a perfect Cullenesque remark ... fame to a little river – not to himself.

'Among his brother artists he had many friends, for with him there were none of those barriers that often mar professional friendships. He was free from prejudices. Though his criticism of the work of others was always sincere and sound, he would, at every opportunity say a constructive word, and found joy in the whole-hearted praise of any achievement deserving it. Students who came to him for help and advice were always sure of a generous and sympathetic response, and the humblest were never scorned.

'We have sat together on the deck of a ship talking under the mid-Atlantic stars; in Paris, at the Dome, with Clarence Gagnon and other friends; at his shack in the Laurentians, and at his studio in Chambly, and he was always the same. His personality transcended environment, or was in harmony with any. He never flashed cheap wit, nor displayed the surface smartness of clever words. He was a nature-lover like Thoreau, seeing in nature not a spectacle, but a revelation through beauty of the oneness of the whole. Thus a daisy could epitomize all flowers, or Mont Tremblant all the mountains of the world. To the critic who said, "I never saw a mountain look like that," he quietly answered, "Perhaps not, but that's the way I did." He would give eyes to the blind, not condemn them for their blindness.

'Our loss is a void in the heart which words are inadequate to express; we have lost one of life's richest treasures ... the perfect friend, Maurice Cullen, who had the power to enrich our lives by the great example of his own.'

5
My Own Exclusive Art Gallery
1921-1932

In 1919, like so many others returned from the war, I felt more 'Canadian' than ever, especially as I soon afterwards, in the following year, married a charming French-Canadian girl, Cécile Bérard. Nearly all my artist friends agreed they felt a strange vitalizing effect on coming home, as if we had found ourselves as Canadians. The smog of our colonialism appeared to have cleared away, we were manufacturing our own goods, and the word 'imported' was beginning to lose its glamour. We had become a nation. Perhaps the firm stand that Sir Arthur Currie had taken during the war had something to do with this, insisting as he did that the Canadian Army should be a separate entity, which of course it became. This was a great contrast with the Boer War, when Canadians were simply British soldiers. And perhaps this growing sense of identity had something to do with my future career and success.

In 1921, following the closing of my father's antique shop on Peel Street, I transferred my collection of paintings into my own gallery. This move to the corner of Bishop and Ste Catherine Streets proved to be justified. The fine firm of Scott and Sons was already established downtown on Notre Dame Street, but they were also frame-makers. I wanted two things – to be uptown, and to deal exclusively in works of art. I thought that Ste Catherine Street West was a good situation. I felt quite confident that with carefully chosen European paintings as a foundation, since no dealer could live on the sale of Canadian art alone,

I would be able to fulfil the dream I had cherished since I walked into John Ogilvy's little gallery sixteen years earlier and asked to see Canadian pictures.

The combination of European and Canadian works in my gallery was essential. There were naturally people who preferred a Corot to a Cullen, or a Boudin to a Brymner. There was international competition in acquiring European paintings, and buying by correspondence was most unsatisfactory. Travel thus was necessary for an art dealer: pictures had to be hunted down, whether at home or abroad. I had good friends in both London and Paris, so the trips to Europe became almost holidays. And while speaking of travel to Europe and my pleasure in it, I should mention the special charm I found in ships.

The somewhat harried plane traveller of today gains time, it is true, but loses much. I fondly recall the comparatively unhurried departure of a ship, with its particular atmosphere and even its smell – the blowing of the bugle or the clanging of the gong, the cry of 'all ashore that's going ashore,' the leisurely farewell, the flowers, the last drink in the cabin, the siren-blast to tell the world we were on our way – and then the slow change of time, the promenade on deck in the sea air, the ship romances to participate in or to watch, and finally to arrive in the same leisurely fashion, suntanned, wide awake, and fit for anything. And think of all those promises we made to meet again.

Between the years 1921 and 1932, I made annual buying trips to Paris, London, and Amsterdam. Amsterdam always seemed sedate after Paris, but I needed the Dutch pictures which were in constant demand in Montreal. Weissenbruch, Bosboom, Anton Mauve, William Maris and Josef Israels were our 'bread and butter,' as many of my customers were still following the advice given by E.B. Greenshields twenty years after the publication of his celebrated book. In Paris I bought pastels by Leon L'Hermitte, paintings by Fantin Latour and Monticelli, Marie Laurencin and Maurice Utrillo, and a great many by Eugène Boudin which I purchased from the firm of Durand-Ruel, who had been his champion. The critics were enthusiastic about our European exhibitions and I always found buyers for the paintings. The *Gazette* of October 14, 1925 had this to say:

At all times a pleasure, perhaps more marked in the delight when chilly winds send scudding clouds that give promise of snow, is looking through the open window of a frame at scenes which suggest smiling peace and warmer airs. Those disturbed by the threat of premature winter can find comfortable solace by dropping into the Watson Art Galleries, 679 St Catherine Street West, where are now on view works by British and Continental painters, brought from Europe by Mr. W.R. Watson.

To the discriminating picture lover the mention of a few names will be sufficient lure – Turner, Constable, Brangwyn, Munnings, Mauve, Blommers, Mesdag, Weissenbruch, Fantin Latour, Henner, Ziem, Boudin, Cazin, L'Hermitte, Jacque, Roybet, Carrière, Harpignies and LeSidaner. All these men, painters of distinction and personal vision in the main, invest their works with a calm so satisfying that, in viewing them, mundane cares can for the nonce be forgotten.

As everyone knows, Paris changed enormously after the Kaiser's war. It quickly became the mecca of the so-called 'lost generation,' and attracted writers and artists from all over the world. Left bank cafés were crowded, and filled with the sense of gaiety that animated people create. I had many happy evenings with Lucile and Clarence Gagnon at the café Dome and the Coupole in Montparnasse, and met many noted artists. There were also memorable summer evenings with the London art dealer Paul Cremetti, who introduced me to his artist friend Jean Louis Forain, at the quieter, more intimate Cascade restaurant in the Bois de Boulogne. For a foreigner, Forain had a remarkable knowledge of Canadian art. He placed Morrice among the greatest artists of the 19th century, and credited him with having influenced some artists in France in the swing away from the extremists among the post-impressionists. He spoke of Maurice Cullen, Suzor Côté, and Clarence Gagnon in a way which showed his familiarity with their works, and he particularly remembered the painting by Cullen which has been purchased by the French government. He also talked about Louis Hemon's *Maria Chapdelaine*, which was being widely read in Paris that year (1924). He thought it gave a somewhat sombre picture of life in northern Quebec, but he spoke of it as a little masterpiece. The book was later illustrated by Clarence Gagnon, who spent more than three years on this task attending to all details; his bright evocative pictures dispelled the sombre impression of Quebec.

Gagnon was the most ebullient of all the artists that I knew with the exception of Suzor Côté. Even his movements seemed quick and energetic, and his chuckling laughter was always at the surface. But he could also concentrate in calmness over long periods of time. For at least two years in succession while living in Paris he did not paint a single picture but worked consistently on the illustrations for *Maria Chapdelaine* – at a loss of many sales to eager would-be buyers of his canvases in Canada. Previous to that, he had concentrated on his etchings, which rank among the very best of that time and had international acclaim. Lucile, his wife, has quoted him as saying, 'To do etchings you need the palm of a duchess and the nerves of a Russian hussar.' Well, he had both. Unfortunately there are not many paintings by Gagnon, and he did not even bother to sign some of them. We sold *Village in the Laurentian Mountains* to the National Gallery of Canada – a church and the old houses he loved. In the background are peaked mountains, not characteristic of the Quebec hills but rather like the Swiss Alps. When I drew his attention to this years later, he laughed, and said, 'What's wrong with that? They've got the best of two worlds.' The mountains must have got into his painting from a sketch made in Switzerland. I am sure nobody objects. Why should they? It's an excellent Gagnon.

Often I wondered if being an art dealer was a business or a hobby – it seemed altogether too enjoyable to be merely a business. There were many amusing moments. One evening at the Dome in Paris, while I was waiting for the Gagnons, a young man sidled up, and in impeccable English said he had heard that I was a Canadian art dealer. He was sure I would be interested in a really great painting that he had – 'a magnificent landscape, a splendid composition, and as bold as any Vlaminck – a gorgeous painting.' 'Who is it by?' I asked nervously. 'By me!' he replied without hesitation. I waved to the approaching Gagnons, and we settled down to our Pernods with yet another story to laugh about. Clarence said I should not have tipped the waiter so much – he was probably a friend of the artist.

I also made frequent trips to London; not only did I find Krieghoff's paintings there, but I also bought more than fifty water colours by the Canadian artist F.A. Verner, who was painting Canadian scenes – Indians, buffalo, and the Alberta prairies – while living in England. He lived there for forty years until he died at over ninety.

In 1924 I went to the British Empire exhibition at Wembley, where Canada had been allocated two rooms in the Palace of Arts. I thought it a great pity that many of our excellent artists were not represented at all. On my return to Montreal I tried to publicize the fact, and urged, through the newspapers, that every effort should be made to make Canada's exhibition more complete and fully representational. It now seems difficult to believe the official prejudice that existed against Canadian landscapes, particularly winter scenes. Perhaps it was considered to be a deterrent to immigration.

It was not always easy to sell Canadian paintings in Montreal in the early days, although Maurice Cullen, Albert Robinson, and briefly J.W. Morrice (when he was painting at Beaupré) were showing us the beauty and character of our winter, and although Eric Brown, director of the National Gallery, had been boldly encouraging such purchases since as early as 1912. Through the newspapers, I also tried to inspire confidence in the potential buyer of works of art, and to thus encourage the sale of works by Canadian artists. In 1922, in an interview with a reporter from the Montreal *Herald*, I said:

> The time is not far off when Montreal will be a leading art centre in the world. It is rightly rated as such at the present time by those who are in touch, but the fact hasn't quite reached the general public yet. Lovers of fine pictures and fine art generally are quiet people as a rule. It might surprise you to know that under the matter-of-fact visage and demeanor of many of our so-called hard-headed business men there lies, or rather seethes, a love and appreciation of beauty known only to the immediate friends and those who act as agents for them.

This message I repeated in other interviews and letters to the editor. Thanks should be given at this point to the attitude of the Montreal press and the help given by them in interesting the public in the work of contemporary Canadian artists. The Montreal *Star* sent the well-known theatre critic Samuel Morgan-Powell to most of our exhibitions and his reviews, good or bad, were always of value as they called attention to the artists' work. *La Presse* also published frequent reviews by Albert Laberge. The *Gazette* had a particularly enthusiastic critic in the person of St George Burgoyne, himself a good amateur painter, a particular lover of the Laurentians, and a great admirer of the work of Maurice Cullen. He came several times to all Cullen's exhibitions for the sheer joy of it, and his criticism was practically always eulogy without stint. For the work of Canadian artists to be considered worthy of newspaper recognition was in itself a significant turn of events. Even those critics who in 1916 were so violently antagonistic to the work of the Group of Seven did an unwitting service to Canadian art; at least they made the public aware of its existence. As a film star once said, 'You can write anything you like about me as long as you mention my name.' Thus the press helped awaken the public to the fact that Canada was producing artists worthy of interest and patronage.

The following are some excerpts taken from the Montreal newspapers of that time. I have kept the clippings all these years.

The Gazette: November 17, 1925
WORKS SHOW RANGE OF GIFTED ARTIST

* * * * *

Oils and Watercolours by William Brymner
Shown at Watson Galleries

* * * * *

Skill, Taste and Sanity
Exhibition Offers Opportunity to Acquire
Pictures Not Likely to Come Soon Again into Market

* * * * *

The Daily Star, November 18, 1925

It has often been cited as a reproach to Canadians that they do not support native artists, but prefer to confine their patronage to foreigners. This charge has been justified within limitations, in the past; but the attitude of the Canadian patron of art has changed materially during the past twenty years. Pictures by Canadian painters today are not ignored, and when they challenge comparison with works by foreign artists, they stand an equal chance with the discriminating purchaser. Today exhibitions of characteristic canvases by men who are in every worthy sense of the word representative of the best in Canadian art my be seen in this city, and will well repay examination.

All the remaining oil paintings and water-colors from the brush of the late William Brymner, C.M.G., R.C.A., have been assembled at the Watson Art Galleries on St. Catherine Street.

The Gazette, March 15, 1926
OILS AND BRONZES BY FACILE ARTISTS

* * * * *

Works by Albert H. Robinson
and
M.A. Suzor Côté
on Exhibit

* * * * *

High Colour-Notes Struck
in Canadian and Other Subjects

* * * * *

Habitant Types in Statuettes

* * * * *

The Gazette, January 20, 1928
LAURENTIAN VISTAS LIMNED BY MASTER

* * * * *

Sixth Annual Exhibition of Maurice Cullen's Works
at Watson Galleries

* * * * *

Artist Maintains his Reputation
as Pre-eminent Interpreter of
Canadian Landscapes Under Snow

* * * * *

The Gazette, January 14, 1929
NORTHLAND SCENES RE-LIVE ON CANVAS

* * * * *

Splendid Examples of Maurice Cullen's Art
Placed on Display at Watson Art Galleries

* * * * *

The Cullen Show is yearly becoming more and more of an event, something that should give infinite satisfaction to W.R. Watson who, a long period ago, without in any measure lessening his appreciation of art from older lands, 'saw something' in Canadian painting, and has sedulously striven to encourage and assist native craftsmen. It was hard sledding in those earlier years – a long spell requiring patience until picture-buyers gradually swung from the placid pastorals of Europe to the cruder, wilder grandeur of Canadian scenes.

During the long depression years, we continued to hold one-man exhibitions for men and women whose work seemed outstanding – not only Cullen but also his stepson Robert Pilot, and Suzor Côté, Albert Robinson, William Brymner, Horatio Walker, and the very good portrait painter Lilias Torrance Newton. By organizing these shows of paintings selected by the artists themselves, we helped to make their work almost popular. We did not hold exhibitions for reasons of sentiment or because of fondness for artist friends, but from belief in the positive worth of their work. Our commission remained 20 per cent on all sales.

Robert Pilot had the subtle charm of natural shyness. It seemed he tried to overcome this by undertaking to do things which were almost the antithesis of his nature – being president of the Arts Club, and later president of the Royal Canadian Academy. Administration and the formalities inherent in such positions were almost painful to him. He called me up one day to say he was leaving his post as president. I said I was glad to hear it. I knew what agonies a speech meant to him. It was he, incidentally, who first suggested, years ago, that I attempt to write this little book.

Pilot was considered exceptional for his time, and was even invited to exhibit with the Group of Seven as early as 1920. As the stepson of Maurice Cullen, and partly his pupil, he lived for some time under a shadow, almost an apprehension, fearing that their styles might be too close. Cullen had never made an etching, so Pilot, to be different, deliberately made eight or ten – nearly all of Quebec City and its surroundings. In my opinion they are among the best etchings ever made in Canada. The prints were extremely limited in number, and now are very scarce.

Bob volunteered and served with distinction in two world wars, and made a considerable contribution as a war artist in England, Italy, and France. He had an excellent command of language, and was a delightful correspondent. His warm-hearted letters reflected the joy of what he was doing and his hope that, as an artist, tomorrow he would do even better.

He had his first one-man exhibition with us in 1927, and it was so successful that he spoke about it for years afterwards. He had no idea that Montreal collectors would be interested in his paintings, believing that they would want only his etchings. He would have been even more surprised to know that in 1969, two years after his death, one of his paintings sold at auction in Montreal for $5,000. This sale may be a tangible indication of what future generations may think of his splendid original technique.

One of my most lively French-Canadian friends for over thirty years was Suzor Côté. He seemed almost indestructible, always the life of the party, bubbling with gaiety and an innate sense of humour – a true Bohemian by nature. Once he came to my gallery with a life-size plaster bust of a proposed 'Maria Chapdelaine' to ask if he should go further with it and have it cast in bronze. He had carried it under his arm all the way from his studio on Ste Famille Street, about a mile away, and he looked for all the world as though he were strangling a young woman. It never occurred to him how sinister he appeared. When I said I thought it was too large for a bronze bust and would be better if smaller, he replied, 'Mon Dieu! you are right!' and dashed it to pieces in my wastebasket. He did make a smaller version later, and it became quite popular.

Suzor Côté had an excellent voice and had thought of being an opera singer. In fact, he had gone to Paris originally to study singing. He returned to Montreal several years after Maurice Cullen, and was certainly influenced by him. But Côté was only a half-way revolutionary. He was not influenced by the Group of Seven, and painted in an almost reticent Barbizon style, mostly around his home in Arthabaska. These paintings have a fundamental sincerity and are always *chez nous*. However, I think he will be remembered principally as a true Quebec sculptor – his formidable *Three Indian Women*, and the famous pair of *Old Pioneers* (old man Cyr and his wife in rocking chairs) will remain as unusual works of essentially Canadian art.

Another artist whom we represented was Albert Robinson. He had come to Montreal from Hamilton, where he was born in 1881, liked the city, and settled permanently there after studying art in Paris. He was a friend of A.Y. Jackson and was often invited to exhibit with the Group of Seven, although he was not a member. I considered him an outstanding colourist, and asked him to paint enough pictures for a one-man show. At the end of a year he was ready, and his exhibition opened on March 15, 1926. He was surprised when we sold eight of the pictures. After it was over I was invited to his house, and over champagne his friends and I proposed a toast to his second show in the following year. Unfortunately we were never able to realize this ambition. He fell into poor health for a considerable time, painted only intermittently, and the few pictures he completed were always quickly sold. He was certainly 'modern,' and even as an individualist was warmly in harmony with the Group of Seven, of which he was an honorary member. None of the Group transcended his paint quality or his fine colour. He is well represented today in the National Gallery of Canada, the Art Gallery of Ontario, and the Art Gallery of Hamilton, but unfortunately not sufficiently so in Montreal. He was one of Canada's finest artists. Jackson himself said, 'I learned a lot from Robinson'.

In the early twenties, in my opinion, no American artist was superior to Maurice Cullen, Tom Thomson, A.Y. Jackson, or Albert Robinson, or even Horatio Walker, whose style was slightly Barbizon. These Canadian artists could hold their own with any of the Hudson River School. We were beginning to overthrow the colonial inferiority complex which had applied to art as well as other endeavours.

Among the most distinguished artists whose work we showed over the years was A.Y. Jackson. He has already written his autobiography in the wide-ranging *A Painter's Country*. We were good friends, but primarily through correspondence, for he did not often visit the city of his birth. However, whenever he came to Montreal he would always find time for a chat in our gallery and sometimes we would lunch together with Arthur Lismer.

Although A.Y. and I exchanged many letters and I sold many of his paintings, in some ways he has been the most elusive of all my artist friends. I think I have an explanation. When he came to Quebec, he did not stay long in Montreal; he was generally in a hurry to get to the country, and especially so in winter. He loved the old Quebec villages and the rolling hills of the Laurentians, and made superb rhythms from them. The charming old churches and solid barns particularly interested him. One of the latter, near the Petite Rivière, was the subject of one of his most popular pictures, *The Red Barn*, painted in 1931, which we bought from him. It is a remarkable painting in many respects, including the technical challenge of using red in the middle distance.

Jackson always looked the picture of health, an essential health like that of a tree. His paintings reflect the man to an unusual degree – vigorous, lively, sincere. But it is difficult to write more about someone who has written his autobiography; when I first read it, it was like shaking hands with him.

A man who seemed to be almost a 'mystery painter' was Horatio Walker, who lived in apparent isolation on the Île d'Orleans from 1883 until his death at eighty years of age. I hardly knew him, but admired his work. He has been called 'the Millet of Canada' with some justification. He painted, in a style reminiscent of the Barbizon school, wood-cutters, habitants standing, hats off, before a wayside cross, and other rural scenes.

The director of the Quebec Museum once asked me to find a representative painting by Walker for the museum. I discovered that for many years a New York art dealer had been buying nearly every picture Walker painted, and I had to secure one through him. Walker represents the quiet introspective side of life as lived in agricultural Quebec, and deserves to be remembered as one of our finest artists. We included his work in group exhibitions, and gave him a one-man show in 1925, but unfortunately his sales were only moderate. However, his paintings were clearly appreciated and purchased by those American art lovers who had come to consider the Barbizon School the paramount art of the day, and in 1929 the enterprising director of the Art Gallery of Toronto managed to locate and bring together enough of his work to hold an exhibition.

Compared to the concentration of painters around Paris and London, Canada's artists were widely separated in these years by the vastness of the country. Montreal, however, enjoyed a cultural awareness in the twenties which was like a renaissance. In Toronto this did not occur until the Mellors Laing Gallery opened in 1931. During the thirties that gallery held exhibitions of the works of the Group of Seven, as well as of J.W. Morrice and David Milne, and became active in selling works by other Canadian artists.

Montreal's cultural awareness was not limited to art, but embraced a great interest in music. In 1930 Montreal still had no concert hall, but in that year Douglas Clarke, Dean of Music at McGill University, and a frequent visitor to our gallery, with infinite courage founded the Montreal Symphony Orchestra. Pulling together many musicians who had been making their livings playing for the silent movies, he soon had them performing Beethoven and Brahms. He even had Gustav Holst as guest conductor, at a performance of one of his compositions, 'The Planets.' The first public concerts were on Sundays at the Orpheum Theatre. My wife and I attended the very first: there were so few people present that Clarke asked everybody to please come down to the stalls where they could be seen. But music lovers rallied around, and the concerts moved to His Majesty's Theatre on Guy Street for several years, often drawing a full house. Later Plateau Hall and then Place des Arts became the orchestra's home.

Douglas Clarke has never been given adequate recognition for what he did for Montreal and its musicians in those critical years as the founder of the Montreal Orchestra. Here is an account of one of those concerts as I described it to the editor of the *Gazette* in 1934.

Sir,–That the Montreal Orchestra would be brilliantly successful, nobody who has followed its upward climb to the front rank can ever have doubted. It has always been a question of how long it could wait for that success to materialize. It has had faith in Emerson's dictum of the maker of mouse-traps, and at last it is about to reap its reward. The Montreal public has rubbed its sleepy eyes and is awake to the fact that it now has an orchestra worth patronizing. It is beating a path to its door. The amazing spectacle at His Majesty's Theatre on Sunday, when the street was blocked with people struggling to get in, so that the concert had to be delayed fifteen minutes, until people were standing in the aisles, and others had to be turned away altogether, was indeed inspiring. But what is more important than the crowd was the enthusiasm displayed for the music heard. Apart from Goluboff's playing, the orchestra itself received rounds of applause (one piece being repeated by insistent demand). Many of the audience were probably hearing it for the first time, and one feels sure that such a joyous afternoon will call them again. The orchestra is going to have crowded houses in the future, so music lovers take the hint if you want to hear it sitting down! The 'Standing Room Only' sign is ready to go out.

I have elsewhere compared Cullen's art to the music of Sibelius. This idea developed from a conversation I once had with Clarke, when he remarked casually that certain paintings seem to have an affinity with music. Rembrandt, he said, suggests Beethoven; Holbein, Bach and Mozart; Monet, Debussy; and Chagall, Stravinsky.

Fortunately, during what has been called the 'terrible years' of the depression, that is from 1929 to 1932, some people continued to buy paintings. The so-called luxury business of selling fine art survived despite popular expectations.

I made a few notes in my day-book of what was happening, and here are some startling stock market facts: Advance Rumley fell from $104 to $3, International Combustion from $103 to $1.50, National Radiator from $98 to $2, White Sewing Machine from $58 to $1, Ajax Rubber from $24 to 25 cents. In two months of steady decline from October to December 1929, a group of fifty-eight stocks plummeted from an average of $57 per share to an average of $1.95. Yet some people still came to our gallery and light-heartedly bought paintings. This gives a good idea of the permanence of art, and even of art values, above almost anything else. The reason is difficult to explain, but perhaps it is simply that good art transcends time and events.

Harry Norton was a constant customer during those years, and I came to rely on him for the certain survival of our business. One day I asked how he managed to keep on buying paintings when there were so many financial ruins about. He told me that he had taken his father's advice and put all his money into bonds, and consequently did not even feel the effect of the market crash. He bought many fine Krieghoffs from us, most of which he later loaned to the Royal Ontario Museum. He also bought paintings during the bottom of the depression by Maurice Cullen, F.S. Coburn and J.W. Morrice. His father had invented the Norton Jack, a railway jack much in use on freight cars throughout North America, and he had inherited the family fortune. He himself did not care for business, but had managed it well until 1920. In that year, having decided to retire, he took a trip to the town of Hell, in Denmark. From there he sent postcards to all his customers with the message, 'I am now in Hell and this is the last time you will hear from me.' Then he sold the business and put the money into those fortunate bonds.

Norton was a great gardener. He loved flowers and lilac trees, and his estate at Ayers Cliff in the Eastern Townships was renowned for its gladioli and peonies. Many of the flowers were magnificent exotic blooms which he created himself through cross-pollination. His house was crowded with paintings by Canadian artists which he collected for love and not as an investment. He was a man of many talents: a botanist, a composer of music, and in all respects a civilized gentleman and a good friend.

Who were some of the other patrons of art in Montreal? Our ledgers, dating from 1910 on, reveal that in the early years most of the buyers of paintings were English Canadians – business and professional men. It was Suzor Côté who said, 'Without you and my English patrons I could never have survived.' But in later years, things began to change, and many more French names appear on the ledger pages.

I have been asked many times, 'Why does the value of an artist's pictures go up after he dies?' A quick answer is, 'Well, the world knows there will be no more of them.' Usually price in art, as in other areas, is determined by supply and demand; an established reputation creates demand, and a death limits supply. Not that the price of a painting is its only value. Ruskin wrote books on art and artists and never mentioned money – except in contempt, as in the court case of Ruskin-Whistler. 'Can you give me the reason or understanding why your painting is worth £200?,' asked the judge in that proceeding. 'I might give you the reason, your Lordship, but not the understanding,' was Whistler's famous answer.

One of the functions of an art dealer as I saw it was to support contemporary artists and encourage them, and to do this in part by taking over the business details involved in the selling of their works, thus allowing them to spend more time in their studios. We delivered and hung the paintings, collected the bills, and were willing, even a year later, to take a picture back, or exchange it for another, if a customer 'could not live with it.' The reputable art dealer is also an adviser, and stands between the public and fraud. There is a wide difference between him and a picture seller. No dealer concerned with reputation would give an exhibition to any artist he thought unworthy, for fear of losing public confidence in his discrimination and judgement.

The public developed confidence in us, and we certainly had confidence in them. People bought paintings, or we sent paintings to their homes on approval for ten days if they wished, with no other surety than the tone of their voice. What man in any other business could say he had never had a bad account in fifty years? As for the stealing of pictures, that seemed unthinkable; we considered them as a white candle in a holy place, immune from the touch of ugly hands. This taken-for-granted honesty on all sides seemed characteristic of the times and added to the pleasantness of life, which was certainly smoother and less hectic than it appears to be today.

After years of assiduously promoting the work of Cullen, Gagnon, Côté, Robinson, and some members of the Group of Seven, the time came when many of our artists were actually pressed with demands for their work. In early January 1931 we sent a cable to Clarence Gagnon in Paris:

> Have a buyer for four of your paintings stop have you anything to send us stop best wishes for new year.

and Gagnon's reply was as follows:

> Sorry nothing available presently happy returns.

In February 1932 we asked A.Y Jackson for as many paintings as he cared to send us. He replied from the Studio Building on Severn Street in Toronto:

> Well you did get something going in Canadian art when you got people to see the great qualities in Cullen.
>
> The problem today is to find enough good paintings to supply the demands. In my own case most of my canvases are being painted to order, and it will take a year for me to be really free.
>
> I don't quite like working that way, and I am sorry that at present I have nothing good enough to send you.

Surely these are fascinating documents. Two Canadian artists in 1932 were sold out and left with 'nothing available.' Who would have thought that possible in 1910? This remarkable letter from Alex Jackson would not have been possible even ten years earlier, when we had difficulty selling a single picture by him.

In May 1932 the lease for my Gallery at 679 Ste Catherine Street West expired, and with short notice my landlord informed me that there would be a considerable increase in rent. I considered such a thing in those difficult times outrageous. My neighbours agreed that it was unjustified, absurd, and entirely out of touch with prevailing conditions. I telephoned the landlord to ask him to reconsider. 'I can make no compromise,' he said. I responded with one of the shortest letters I ever wrote:

Dear Sir:

In reply to your letter of etc., I shall not require these premises after May 15th.

Yours truly,

Those who care to unravel the happenings in their lives can perhaps find climactic moments like this, when apparent injury done to them becomes a future blessing, or when ten seconds of decision changes the whole of their future lives. This was just such an occasion. I held a ten-day sale of paintings, sent the rest to storage, and on May 12, 1932, we closed the gallery.

That summer we went to our cottage in the country. I was a man without a business. I should have been worried and unhappy but I was not. I was having months of compulsory holiday with my wife and daughters and never enjoyed the country more. We bought a 'Snipe' class sailboat and explored the beautiful lake for the first time. We studied flowers and noted the bird songs that made May and June an enchantment. The Cullens visited us with Bob Pilot, and we talked through sunsets into starlight, 'about it and about.' It was a happy summer.

6
The First Art Gallery on Sherbrooke Street West
1932-1958

One day in September, while we were still living in the country, a friend who was a real estate agent telephoned from Montreal. 'Are you going to open again, Bill? Have you found premises? I've just heard of a building for sale on Sherbrooke Street. It would make an excellent gallery.' I went to Montreal, saw the rather handsome building on the south side of the street between Bishop and MacKay, had a fair vision of Sherbrooke becoming the local equivalent of New York's Fifth Avenue, and promptly bought the building for $30,000. It had formerly been a private residence, and as part of the necessary renovation we installed a show window of generous vertical dimensions, faced with marble. A big gallery occupied the ground floor, which was finished in silver grey, with an office in the rear. Upstairs was another gallery, with a show room behind it. That floor was also finished in grey, slightly different in tone, but as below designed to provide restful, neutral surroundings for the enjoyment of paintings. Thus began the first commercial art gallery on Sherbrooke Street West.

We opened on December 7, 1932, with an exhibition which included paintings by A.Y. Jackson, Albert Robinson, Maurice Cullen, Suzor Côté, Robert Pilot, and Horne Russell, plus European paintings by Pissarro, Boudin, Vlaminck, and Utrillo. From the response to that first exhibition, I felt assured there was no mistake in this pioneering move uptown. In those days Sherbrooke Street was essentially residential and comparatively quiet; cars could park an unlimited time outside the gallery, a very important consideration of which our customers took full advantage. As one indication of the immense change in Sherbrooke since then, today it is illegal even to stop one's car in that location. There are, of course, many galleries and exclusive shops there now.

By this point it is becoming clear that in writing my reminiscences as an art dealer, I am in effect writing about my artist friends, for they were the leit-motif of my career. It would be delightful if I had the capacity to write a biography of each one, but I must be content with only brief references to those who drift into my mind when I think about the past.

One of the most cherished and unusual men I knew during those fifty years was Marius Barbeau. I say 'knew,' although perhaps nobody really did, for Barbeau was so versatile and many-faceted in his personality and tastes that he seemed to be a different man every time one met him. His interests were far-reaching, and his literary works have had an important influence.

He was associated with the National Museum of Canada from about 1911 on, and apparently had a great deal of freedom to do what he liked. In 1912 he wrote his first book on the mythology of the Huron Indians of Quebec and in 1961 one of his last on Tsimsyan Indian myths of the West coast. In the interim he wrote more than forty books – the titles almost encyclopaedic in range. His knowledge of Indian languages, arts, crafts, songs, and even myths, was remarkable. Once I asked him whom he considered the greatest artist in Canada. Half-humorously he said, 'It's a group, long before the Group of Seven – the Haida Indians.'

Canada owes a profound debt of gratitude to Barbeau. He knew his beloved Quebec best – its farmhouses, churches, the decorative arts, crafts, songs, and folklore, which he recorded on the spot and about which he wrote extensively. On the West coast he ferreted out the best remaining totem poles and stayed long enough to study and write *Haida Myths*. Did anybody know the geography, and perhaps more importantly, the spirit and soul of this country better than he? I do not think he would have cared to think of himself as a bronze statue, but there are monuments on this continent to men who did far less than Barbeau to justify them. And how would a sculptor depict such a man?

In 1934 I had the pleasure of working with him on his book about

Krieghoff. During that time he talked a great deal about a White-Indian theme which has been in his mind for years. It sounded interesting, and I asked, 'When we've finished the Krieghoff hunt and you've written the book and cleared the decks, will you settle down and write that "great Canadian novel".' He quietly said 'I might.' The subject was never mentioned again, but ten years later, in 1944, I received in the mail a three-hundred page book inscribed to me as 'friend and most cheerful reader.' It was his novel *Mountain Cloud*, a book unfortunately almost unknown today, strangely Indian in its rhythms.

Barbeau was delightful company, speaking his Oxford English with me, and his impeccable French with my wife, Cecile. We once got on to the subject of Indian songs and singing. 'Please, Marius, do sing us an Indian song,' we asked. 'I can't do that in silence,' he said. 'I need a certain kind of noise and I know where I might find what I need.' He went into the kitchen and came out with two saucepan lids. On that warm summer evening we sat on the balcony, while Barbeau, off in a kind of trance, clanged those lids together like cymbals, and sang Huron and other Indian songs to us for more than half an hour. A full moon, filtered through a near-by tree, shone on his face as he sang with his eyes half closed. That is how I most vividly remember him. What a pity there is no other record of that enchanting time.

In the new gallery we also had exhibitions of European paintings lent by Durand-Ruel and Jacques Dubourg of Paris, and, later, of work by Harold Beament, F.W. Hutchison, and many others. These artists also became my friends.

One-man exhibitions were always exciting, especially when they were successful and one had the pleasure of handing the artist a sturdy cheque he deserved. If the exhibition had been a failure, the artist sometimes compensated by assuring us 'it was a great *succès d'estime'* – a phrase which always touched my heart. At many of our exhibition openings we served champagne and there was much gaiety and laughter.

One of the artists whose work we consistently showed during these years was Harold Beament. He is still one of my oldest friends – an artist, sailor, bon vivant, and humorist. We both know the difference between a knot and a mile. Harold served in the navy in two world wars, and was eventually my senior in rank although junior in age. I suspect that he had a better time of it in the first world war when he was a warrant officer. In the second, he had command of a ship on the cold North Atlantic patrol. I received a letter from him written at sea somewhere north of Halifax, expressing his feeling that it was 'a young man's war.' After nearly three years of active service among mine sweepers and escort vessels, he was appointed senior naval war artist.

Harold had the remarkable ability to drop his brushes for months and pick them up again with renewed interest. He had an intellectual approach to painting – once, for example, he brought me a painting of a great iceberg, cleverly scaled by a diminutive kayak with one Eskimo in it – yet his art remained quite personal. He always maintained that Eskimos were 'happy people' and he portrayed them with rosy cheeks and smiling faces. Not long ago he received special recognition by being elected president of the Royal Canadian Academy. I would very much have liked to have heard him make his first speech, since he is a witty man. We had many lunches together at the Epicurean Club restaurant on Sherbrooke Street near my gallery, where he would lie in wait to test me with crossword puzzles and the stimulus of a sharp mind and wit.

One of the most intellectual artists I knew was John Lyman, who was a great admirer of Matisse and showed that influence in many of his pictures. I always regretted not being able to arrange a complete exhibition of his work. Lyman spent a good deal of his time writing essays and articles on art, and through his criticism and lectures did much to bring about a better conception of what 'living art' was and could be in Canada. One summer at North Hatley I had the pleasure of sitting beside him while he painted, and was surprised at how disciplined each brush-stroke appeared. He quite obviously enjoyed painting. Like his friend J.W. Morrice, who was twenty-one years his senior, Lyman had independent means, and apparently painted only for the pleasure of creation. He was completely bilingual, and thus formed a link between the two cultures in the artistic world of the province. He founded the Contemporary Art Society, and there is a room in the Quebec Museum dedicated to him.

During this period I continued to take every opportunity to maintain confidence in the purchase of paintings and in particular to encourage the interest in Canadian art. In 1935 I wrote an article for the *Gazette* which reflected my feelings:

A SECRETARY OF ARTS?

We have had occasion during the past years to refer to the universal and growing interest in art. We have mentioned the enormous crowds that thronged the various exhibitions in London, New York and Paris. There is now a bill before The Congress of the United States to form a new department with a Secretary of Arts.

The preamble to this bill declares 'whereas in the opinion of the best informed men and women of the United States "man shall not live by bread alone," and that there is more to life and living than the solely material things of existence, and that visions, without which the people perish, and beauty and ideals, are as essential to the promotion of the general welfare as are the things of substance.'

In Canada, the private citizen is showing a decided and growing interest in all that pertains to art, but it will apparently be a long time before such a trend crystallizes to the extent of reaching parliament. But new life-values are being evolved in our consciousness, and we are discovering that art is a verity that never disillusions, and that 'beauty is truth.'

Fortunately Montreal is already rich in art treasures, and our Art Gallery is ready to respond to public demands. Our National Gallery is awake to the new renaissance, and several important travelling exhibitions have been shown in the principal cities. We are sharing in the world movement towards the things that are more excellent. It is all to the good. But when shall we have a 'Secretary of Arts'?

In 1933 I wrote a letter to the *Gazette*:

Sir, – Your editorial on 'Life and Art' was admirable as it was apt. That 34,000 people should visit the Van Horne collection is a local example of the great and apparently growing interest in art.

For those who can afford them, paintings in the home are one of the great pleasures of life, and for those who cannot indulge in possession, there are the galleries and museums. How much a solace to the pre-occupied modern mind works of art can be, is perhaps well described in the following quotation ...

'Pictures are loopholes of escape to the mind, leading it to other scenes and spheres, as it were through the frame of an exquisite picture, where the fancy for the moment may revel, refreshed and delighted. Pictures are the consolers of loneliness; they are a sweet flattery to the imagination; they are a relief to the jaded mind; they are windows to the imprisoned thought; they are Books, they are Histories and Sermons. They make up for the want of many other enjoyments to those whose life is mostly passed amidst the smoke and din, the bustle and noise of an over-crowded city.'

Here perhaps is the best explanation of the whole movement towards art as a relief from the encroaching materialism of our age. It is the cry of halt to the threatened obliteration of all that is intrinsically beautiful in life; and without a sense of beauty man is little better than a robot. The artist, more than at any time in history, perhaps has an important place in the scheme of life, and to him the world looks with an hungered soul for that continuous revelation of the beauty that lurks in everything. He will show us the world's eternal youth, and maintain our sense of joy and wonder in it.

One artist who always impressed me with his interpretations of the beauty of the Lower St Lawrence region was Fred Hutchison. He was well known in the art world of both Canada and the United States, but unfortunately his works are not well represented in Quebec, the province in which he was born and which he particularly loved. Although lured by circumstances to live for years in New York, where he taught art during the winter, he never failed to make the annual pilgrimage to his house at Baie St Paul. From there he painted vital landscapes of that region, including the hinterlands of Charlevoix county, an area that no member of the Group of Seven had yet discovered. Like Cullen, he was a sincere individualist, but while Cullen invariably painted the Laurentians in winter, Hutchison much preferred their summer and autumn aspects. Thus we have from these two artists the beauty of changing seasons. Hutchison's character as a man was well reflected in his painting. His was a calm, quiet personality, yet tremendously and completely outgoing. He was fond of golf in summer and of outdoor curling in winter, and was adept as well at billiards.

Hutchison was one of the first of our outdoor painters: I once had to take the sand out from behind a large canvas stretcher. Even his largest pictures have the freshness of sketches. Fortunately some directors recognized his significance and he is fairly well represented in Canadian galleries, and the Americans also have good examples of his work.

Another friend and constant visitor to our gallery was Frederick S. Coburn, whose still life, *Roses in a Bowl*, was the first Canadian painting I sold, back in 1906. He favoured the Eastern Townships near Melbourne, where he was born, and more than half his pictures are winter logging scenes painted entirely in his studio. He began painting such pictures about 1910. They became so popular that someone said, 'It looks as if every house should have a piano and a Coburn.' Displayed in our window, they would invariably sell on the same day. Only a fortunate laziness prevented Coburn from over-doing it altogether.

Coburn lived to be eighty-nine, and always gave the impression of being slow-paced, quiet-spoken, and apparently unworried by anything in the world. His early manhood had been spent in poverty, especially his student days in Antwerp when a bowl of soup was often his food for a day. He never really recovered from that period, and was reluctant to spend money on himself or to indulge in almost normal creature comforts. He once came into the gallery complaining of feeling ill, and I had to insist that he go home in a taxi. He thought of it as a waste of money.

Coburn discovered the effectiveness of a brown horse against a white one, or vice-versa, as a perfect complement. Once he rented a horse from a farmer in Melbourne to make drawing studies. The farmer came to see what work his horse was being required to perform, and found it tethered in the artist's back yard, doing nothing. 'I just want to look at it,' said Coburn. The farmer must have thought he was some kind of crackpot. But no painter in Canada knew working horses better, and his logging scenes were what he saw in the wooded hills of the Townships which he loved. He painted with sincerity and a deliberate realism which was probably why his paintings were so popular and easily understood. The interest in them has continued. A new generation has paid as much as $5,000 for a *Logging Scene* that we sold originally for $450.

After we had occupied the Sherbrooke Street premises for seven years, the second world war broke out. This time I was too old to volunteer, and so I carried on in business. The war did not affect the sale of paintings very much; we continued to hold exhibitions and people still sought advice on the purchase of paintings. It was a very special pleasure occasionally to find a collection that clearly revealed the owner's taste and knowledge. I had such an experience in 1940.

I was asked to evaluate a small collection of paintings, for which the Ottawa owner was trying to obtain insurance for $75,000. Some of the artists' names interested me, and I agreed to go on behalf of the insurance company. The owner lived in a small apartment and he let me in himself. I asked him to please leave me alone while I did my appraisal. The pictures were in his living room, bedrooms, and den, and I was astonished at what I saw. There were sixteen paintings altogether, and ranged from Corot to Pissarro. Every one seemed of superlative quality, and I felt like a man drinking champagne. I took my time, out of sheer enjoyment.

I calculated my valuation on the prices I could get for the pictures, on the basis of telephone calls to agents I knew in New York. When I totalled the figures, the amount came to over $240,000. I think I told the owner this with a tremor in my voice. That was a great deal of money in those days. He did not seem in the least surprised. He said, 'I know, I know, Mr. Watson. I think you are very close. I am willing to take a heavy chance with my insurance coverage – perhaps too much of a chance.' I asked where he had acquired such an excellent collection and what provenance or documents he had concerning them. 'I have not kept any invoices or papers whatsoever. That is why I want an insurance listing.' Then followed this remarkable story.

He had been a very prosperous silk merchant in Germany. When Hitler was beginning to make things difficult for the Jewish people, he became convinced that the situation would get worse and decided to leave the country forever. From the moment of that decision German money meant nothing to him, but he desperately wanted to save his paintings. Yet he did not know how to take them with him, since it was illegal to export works of art.

Taking a fearful risk, he gave an enormous bribe (in German marks) to a high-ranking Nazi officer. Arrangements were then made, and through a series of complicated manoeuvres his entire collection was delivered in four neat packages to his son in Zurich. A few months later the father arrived in Switzerland as a German expatriate.

After this story, I asked if I could go around the collection once more. I did so with a continuing sense of amazement and appreciation of his good taste and good luck. His cleverness and courage extended well beyond the saving of his precious art collection, for he also managed to take much of his fortune out of Germany, when to take out anything more than fifty dollars was a serious crime. He accomplished this by transferring all his German money into shares of good, available American stocks, sometimes paying double the price in order to get them. He then arranged for a well-known London lawyer to come to his home in Berlin, bringing an assistant with him. After lunch the London solicitors, with their host, sat around a cheerful fire, with cognac and cigars. They discussed a strange assignment: the Englishmen were to witness and record the burning of all his stock certificates. One by one the documents were burned to ashes in that fire – a sort of financial orgy – while the lawyers made records in their notebooks. Later, in New York, with his 'documents of witnessed destruction,' he was able to secure re-issues of all the certificates.

It will be seen that one of the greatest pleasures of being an art dealer was the number of interesting people thus met who often became friends. There was an art language and an art literature, and paintings to be studied in different parts of the world, and after fifty years I always felt there was a great deal more to learn. In my time I have seen many art movements develop – Dadaism, Cubism, Expressionism, Abstract Art, Surrealism, and the Automatistes. One might well ask, what next? However, the dedicated dealer buys and sells only what he believes in, or what he considers to be art. Many people consider themselves to have an instinctive flair and enjoy the fun of relying on their own judgement, and to them one can only say, 'Good luck.' I am proud to recall the names of artists whose work we recommended fifty years ago – Krieghoff, Morrice, Cullen, Robinson, Jackson, Gagnon, Suzor Côté, and many others. As I look through photographs and read press reports on sales, I can hardly believe what has happened to their value, although I must admit I half expected it.

We were constantly asked for advice on the purchase of paintings, but it was not always taken. Art dealers have an amusing saying of unknown origin, 'Beware of the early morning buyer.' One morning I was confronted by a gentleman who seemed particularly cheery and affable. He asked if I was Mr Watson, and when I said I was, he began with a line of flattery. 'I've been recommended to take your advice, and they say you are in every way reliable. I want three particularly good paintings for the living room of my new house.' Just a few days before we had received from Paris three paintings by J.W. Morrice. They were so excellent I had been admiring them in the privacy of the showroom: *Yacht Race St Malo*, *The Luxembourg Gardens*, and a charming snow scene, *Return from School*. I told him that we had just received some very special paintings and he came upstairs to see them. He looked closely at each one, and suddenly said, 'Do you really recommend those things to me at over $1,000 each? Preposterous! Such sloppy work, not a detail anywhere!' He was getting red in the face as he turned to me, and in real anger said, 'Mr Watson ... *reliable be damned*!' I had no time to say another word as he stomped down the stairs and out through the door.

There have been numerous references to the value of paintings in these random reminiscences, and I make no excuses for them. I never thought of paintings as things to buy like stocks and it was only when I saw the rise in their cost that this phase of dealing in art became apparent to me. It has been one of life's surprises, and a pleasant one.

It would be impossible to ignore all the people who came from Europe and asked me to look at paintings that they had acquired by the greatest good luck, 'White Russian treasures that were smuggled out for a quick and secret sale.' There were several variations, but 'White Russian treasure' and 'secret sale' invariably meant fraud. There were also heavy losses in buying 'Corots' and 'Millets' that had probably been painted in the Paris suburbs. On account of this I cannot resist giving some advice: 'If you want to buy pearls, go to a reputable jeweller; if it is paintings you want, go to a reputable art dealer, or to an artist's studio.' One of the oldest art jokes is, 'Yes, this is a picture by —— and it was painted by him while he was alive.' This says almost everything about fraud one need know – always remembering, too, that the little signature in the corner may mean nothing.

Many otherwise astute people are victims of the romantic world of art. A kind of miasma comes over their minds with the jargon of the studio, and the stories they have heard of Rembrandts and Rubens that were bought for a song after being 'discovered' in some old garret. But most people are naturally discerning enough to patronize established dealers, and for some, buying paintings is a paramount part of living and of making their home a more beautiful environment.

Although dealing in art was fundamentally a business, there was always the possibility of exciting discoveries, and also an element of gambling, for you had no idea who might like the paintings you had chosen. One also met frequent requests for valuations, with pleasant surprises for some owners at least. Sometimes the results were most unexpected. An elderly woman once came into the gallery with a small picture wrapped in newspaper. 'What can you give me for this? I badly need some money,' she said. I found it to be a sketch of an Indian head done on note-paper by Paul Kane. 'I badly need some money' echoed in my ears, so I decided to give her the maximum I could afford. 'I will give you $1,000 for it,' I told her. She promptly fainted. When she had recovered with the help of a little brandy, she said she had expected $25 or less. The name of the artist meant absolutely nothing to her, but a happy woman left the gallery that day.

Then there was the other side, the bitter disillusionment of the bargain hunters, especially people who bought pictures from hearsay. A man once came in to show me a Krieghoff he had acquired. He was positive and enthusiastic: 'They told me it had been in the same family since Krieghoff's time. Besides that, it's signed,' and he thought that the signature ought to settle my obvious doubts. I agreed with him that the picture was signed, but by *C. KREIGHOFF*. That transposed *E* and *I* tripped up more than one forger in my day.

Another story about a signature is also worth recounting, perhaps as a warning. I was asked over the telephone if I could value a portrait by Sir Joshua Reynolds. 'Who is it of?' I asked. 'I don't know,' said the lady, 'but it is of a gentleman and fully signed Joshua Reynolds.' 'Then I don't need to see it,' I replied. 'Why not?' she asked. I explained that so far as I knew Sir Joshua Reynolds had signed only one picture in all his life, the portrait of the famous actress Mrs Siddons as *The Tragic Muse*. As he signed it, he is known to have said, 'Madame, you see I shall go down to posterity on the hem of your garment.'

As an art dealer my contact with the public held further continuing interest. The genuine art lovers were charming to meet, and every day held the possibility of some pleasant encounter or intellectual stimulation. My customers were varied, and the selling of a painting often involved many hours of conversation. I thus learned many things. They included politicians, businessmen, civil servants, and members of many professions; and in the late nineteen forties and fifties, many more of them than in the past were French-Canadian. One of these was the Honourable Maurice Duplessis, then premier of Quebec, who spent many of his weekends away from the Legislature at the Ritz Carlton Hotel on Sherbrooke Street. On a Saturday morning he would often come into our gallery for a visit. He was keenly interested in art, and seemed to relax and enjoy himself in our upstairs showroom. He especially liked paintings by Krieghoff, Gagnon, Côté, Walker, painters of the Barbizon School, and the 19th century artists Corot and Jongkind. Many paintings from our gallery are now part of the Province of Quebec's collection as a result of Duplessis's interest.

Of course there was also the occasional fool. Every art dealer, I imagine, has had to deal with the odd character who says such things as: 'Are these all hand-painted paintings?' 'Are the rough ones the expensive ones?' 'I think that's very cheap for $9.50. … Oh, you mean nine hundred and fifty!' 'I know nothing about art, but I know what's good.' 'It seems to me, some paintings are better than they look.' 'I would like a painting to go with a green rug and pink cushions.' 'Are you *the* Mr Watson? Then did you paint all these pictures?'

There was as well a light-hearted side to dealing with artist friends and other dealers – the humorous studio talk that most in our circles are familiar with, stories of the art world, some of them classic. Here are some that appeal to me.

A visitor to Whistler's studio pointed out a passage he liked, and in so doing smudged it with his fingers. 'Oh, that's too bad,' said Whistler, 'the paint was wet.' 'Never mind,' said the visitor, 'I had my gloves on.' And on another occasion, 'I'm not so sure it's a great work of art,' said a very conceited sitter. 'Perhaps you're not exactly a great work of nature,' was Whistler's acid reply.

Sir William Orpen was once asked by a potential sitter, 'Sir William, how do you mix your colours?' 'With brains,' was the quiet answer.

My own story, one that artists particularly seemed to appreciate, was about a meeting with the portrait painter John Sargent in London shortly after the first world war. I inquired about his work. 'Yes, I'm still doing war work,' he said. 'I'm painting a group of ten military officers and their twenty bloody boots.'

Greuze, as we all know, painted sweetly beautiful children. He had two quite homely children of his own. An over-candid friend said, 'It's too bad, Jean, that you who paint such beautiful children should not have had beautiful children of your own.' 'But there's a difference my dear friend,' said Greuze. 'When I'm painting, I can see what I'm doing.'

I enjoyed sharing such jokes with my customers. An artist friend who also loved a joke was Arthur Lismer. He had a great sense of humour. Like his younger friend Frederick Varley, he was born in Sheffield, England. Lismer went to Toronto about 1911, and came to Montreal in 1940. Although he was one of the early members of the Group, I have always wished that he had painted more. He became a teacher in the Montreal Museum of Fine Arts, and was nothing less than a genius with the children who were his students there. He believed in 'creative child art' and the youngsters adored him. The museum being just across the street from our gallery, he came to most of our exhibitions and sometimes brought in a class of students. On occasion we lunched with our mutual friend, Barbeau, and then the conversation truly sparkled.

As business establishments began to move in along Sherbrooke Street, the old residents began to move away from the increasingly busy street. Unfortunately, this caused some developments that were not to our liking – fine old houses with signs advertising 'Rooms to Let,' and in other houses a general appearance of deterioration.

One of my friends and customers was François Dupré, who had recently bought the Ritz Carlton Hotel. He agreed that many of the signs were eye-sores and that something should be done about it. I had heard of the Fifth Avenue Association in New York, which had done marvels to preserve the dignity of that street. I got in touch with them, and explained our situation. They were very helpful, even sending us a copy of their charter. In 1950 we decided to form a Sherbrooke Street Association on the same lines. We had a meeting of property owners and tenants who were interested and I was elected president, with

Frank McKenna of McKenna's House of Flowers as vice-president. Our board room was in the Ritz Carlton Hotel, courtesy of Mr Dupré, who bought several Canadian paintings from me for its walls.

What we did was almost fantasy. We had no legal powers to implement our requests, no powers at all in fact, but we were able to prompt action – perhaps only by our impressive note paper and impertinent language. Letters went out with such messages as, 'At a meeting of our Association, your protruding "Rooms to Rent" sign was considered to be a violation of our by-laws, and you are hereby requested to remove it within ten days from the receipt of this letter.' Strange as it may seem, most recipients complied with our demands. One newspaper reported us as a 'militant group intending to stoutly oppose over-commercialism and the erection of unsightly signs, buildings or shops.' This sort of publicity may have contributed to our pursuasiveness, for a great improvement in Sherbrooke Street's appearance took place. Holt Renfrew already had a fine building, and the Ritz Carlton Hotel made an addition to theirs. Then a few of the older houses were converted into attractive stores such as Brisson and Brisson (gentlemen's apparel), Trevor Peck (high fidelity equipment), Gabriel Lucas Limitée (jewellery), John Russell (fine antiques), and others. This suggests what can be done by comparatively simple means – let us say, by a kind of moral persuasion. I also had great confidence then in the cultural future of Montreal and in the pride of its citizens.

In 1950, my elder daughter Claire joined me at the gallery. We already had two honest and devoted men in Benny and Archie Grant, brothers who had become well known to our clients. They both loved paintings and enjoyed their work. As Claire had grown up in the world of art and was an excellent organizer, we were able to keep extremely active with one-man shows of work by Canadian artists. These included Lorne Bouchard, John Little, John Fox, and York Wilson, who had their first exhibitions with us. We also exhibited and sold paintings by Philip Surrey, John Lyman, Harold Beament, Robert Pilot, Goodridge Roberts, Stanley Cosgrove, Alex Colville, Frank Hennessey, and Adrien Hebert. From the first, Claire fully appreciated many of the contemporary Canadian artists, and had a large part in arranging exhibitions of their work. It was a pleasure for me to see such enthusiasm in another generation.

Altogether, the atmosphere of that Sherbrooke Street gallery was always pleasant, with the pictures being shown as they would be seen in any home. For the first four years we had used the gallery as our family home; the top floor was an apartment, and the second floor gallery was our living-room 'after hours.' Claire recalls seeing an exhibition of paintings by J.W. Morrice in London in 1968, in which at least five of the works were familiar living-room pictures of her childhood. My younger daughter Louise recalls childhood parties held in our gallery home with paintings by Modigliani, Monet, Renoir, Toulouse Lautrec, and Utrillo on the walls. (This was the collection brought to Canada by Jacques Dubourg of Paris for an exhibition.) Later, when the family moved into a new house, we took over the entire gallery building for our business. The second floor bathroom was transformed into an unusual bar, with amusing red curtains and dozens of photographs of Canadian artists on the walls. At certain times the near-by 'show room' became transformed into a comfortable lounge, and we spent enjoyable hours there with innumerable friends and artists, as well as art dealers from Canada and abroad. It seemed that being an art dealer could never be ponderous or solemn, for art represented an aspect of life in which smiles were more usual than frowns. These were happy years in all respects.

I had always felt that other art dealers would support artists of their day with the same conviction I had had in the twenties. One such person was the courageous Agnes Lefort, who opened her own little gallery on Sherbrooke Street at Peel in November 1950, and moved in 1952 to Sherbrooke Street West near Guy Street. With great integrity and dedication she supported with fair success the avant-garde artists of the time such as Paul Emile Borduas and his followers. Montreal owes much to her perception and spirit. In Toronto the Laing Galleries also did much to promote Canadian art and also held annual exhibitions of modern European paintings.

During the last ten years of business on Sherbrooke Street, we appreciated our association with the firm of E.J. van Wisselingh & Co. of Amsterdam. This long established and highly reputable gallery was being managed by Peter Eilers, Jon De Jong, and his son Niko De Jong. For a decade, from 1948 to 1958, we sponsored their annual exhibitions of important paintings by classic and modern European artists of distinction. Much as I appreciated and promoted the work of our own Canadian artists, these fine shows were assurance that we would never succumb to a narrow chauvinism, and added to our own reputation as a consequence.

From these exhibitions, the National Gallery of Canada bought many paintings, brought to its attention by the astute director, H.O. McCurry. Among them were August Renoir's *Claude et Renée*, Paul Gauguin's *Paysage à Pont Aven*, Pierre Bonnard's *Le Port de Cannes*, and two flower pictures by Vincent Van Gogh. Private collections were also greatly enriched, and during the two weeks of these annual exhibitions our gallery was alive with keen and enthusiastic art lovers and collectors. Many fine paintings consequently remained in Montreal.

I have lived long enough to be aware of what has happened to the art and the artists I believed in. Two London auction firms are now represented in Canada: Christie's in Montreal and Sotheby & Co. in Toronto. Since 1969 they have held several sales of Canadian paintings, and the keen competition to acquire these works has been like a tonic to my ego, something very pleasant in retirement, for perhaps it justifies my judgement and advice. The following are some of the prices paid: Robert Pilot's *Farmouse in Quebec*, 17 × 23 inches, sold for $4,000; Maurice Cullen's *March Thaw*, 24 × 30 inches, sold for $7,500; Arthur Lismer's *Country Garden*, 11½ × 15½ inches, sold for $2,800; Albert Robinson's *Winter in the Hills*, 26 × 33 inches, sold for $19,000; Cornelius Krieghoff's *Huron Indians at Camp*, 11½ × 15½ inches, sold for $14,000, and his *Indian Hunters*, 12¾ × 17¾ inches, sold for $22,000; A.Y. Jackson's *Quebec Village Winter*, 21 × 23 inches, sold for $16,500; Lawren Harris's *End of Lake in Algoma*, 10 × 14 inches, sold for $9,000; J.W. Morrice, a panel, 9 × 12 inches, sold for $8,000; and a third Krieghoff, an oval *Portrait of John Budden*, sold for $25,000.

On the wall of a London artist's studio I once saw these Latin words: 'Ars Longa, Vita Brevis.' After more than fifty years as an art dealer, and writing in my eighty-fifth year, I can only say, '... how true.' There will be other artists with messages and personal styles, and other art dealers who will have confidence in them, to show their work in galleries for generations to come.

To have been an exclusive art dealer for over fifty years was certainly one of life's privileges, and I am profoundly grateful for it. In 1958, at seventy-one years of age, I decided to close the Watson Art

Galleries. My daughter Claire realized how emotional an experience it was going to be for me and valiantly took over this rather complicated undertaking. Claire realized as well as I did that we were closing a very successful gallery out of choice and not under any kind of compulsion, and that made the atmosphere more pleasant than it might have been. Nothing in life is ever as bad as it could be.

When our gallery was finally closed and I had announced my retirement, I received many letters from patrons and artist friends, some of which were like condolences, and others generous with flattery. I gladly conclude this story of my years as an art dealer with one of these letters, which seemed as sincere as the paintings of the man who wrote it. It was from A.Y. Jackson:

> My Dear Watson:
>
> So you are retiring from business and going to spend the rest of your days sitting in the sun – reading – fishing, and I hope writing your reminiscences, all the things you could only do at odd times during your busy life. You have known, and been a good friend to nearly all the artists, and must have happy memories of many of them. I share in the general feeling of regret that you will no longer be carrying on, and I wish you happiness in the years ahead.

Well, friend Jackson, you and Robert Pilot are partly responsible for what I have tried to do. I know that I have written without absolute sequence, but with a steady enjoyment, all of which seems rather the way I have lived: a life of much happiness.

Index

Unless otherwise noted, street names and buildings are in Montreal

www.ingramcontent.com/pod-product-compliance
Lightning Source LLC
LaVergne TN
LVHW040759070826
844660LV00025B/1196

* 9 7 8 1 4 8 7 5 8 5 7 3 0 *